Cookbooking
the delicious new way to scrapbook

sixth&spring books

233 Spring Street
New York, New York 10013

Editorial Director
ELAINE SILVERSTEIN

Book Division Manager
WENDY WILLIAMS

Senior Editor
MICHELLE BREDESON

Art Director
DIANE LAMPHRON

Associate Art Director
SHEENA T. PAUL

Book Design
NANCY SABATO

Copy Editor
KRISTINA SIGLER

Vice President, Publisher
TRISHA MALCOLM

Production Manager
DAVID JOINNIDES

Creative Director
JOE VIOR

President
ART JOINNIDES

Library of Congress Control Number: 2008925014

ISBN-13: 978-1-933027-38-8
ISBN-10: 1-933027-38-X

Manufactured in China

1 3 5 7 9 10 8 6 4 2

First Edition

Cookbooking

the delicious new way to scrapbook

BARBARA WINKLER

Contents

8. Introduction

So what is this thing called "cookbooking"?

10. On the Road

A memento-packed travelogue, starring meals inspired by trips

RECIPES Classic Gazpacho • Mussels with White Wine, Butter and Garlic

22. Down Memory Lane

Recipes and reminiscences bound together with love

RECIPES Broccoli Salad • Sour Cream Raisin Pie

33. The Littlest Chefs

Kid-tested dishes in a kid-friendly format

RECIPES Frozen Fruity Yogurt Pops • Peewee Pizza

42. Where's Dinner?

Simple suppers reinvented

RECIPES Lemon Herb Lamb • Fish Baked in Foil

54. Home for the Holidays

The food, the folks, the fun of the holidays, all in a keepsake book

RECIPES
- Roast Turkey with Herbs and Herb Butter
- Spinach Salad with Pears and Cranberries
- Cornbread, Mushroom and Pancetta Stuffing
- Roasted Sweet Potatoes

66. Crazy for Chocolate!

An ode to the most sensuous of ingredients

RECIPES Chocolate-Apricot Tart • Grandma's Mistakes

76. Shaken, Not Stirred

No-fail party drinks in an easy
foldout guide

RECIPES
- The Ultimate Margarita
- Punch with a Punch
- Pomegranate Martini

84. Rise 'n' Shine

An at-the-ready stash to start
the day off right

RECIPES Huevos Rancheros
- French Toast with Baked Bananas

92. To Your Health

This shape-up primer is a guide,
journal and recipe file all in one

RECIPES Fruit Slushy • Pepper Medley

102. Thrills from the Grill

Best of the best barbecue dishes

RECIPES Asian Grilled Swordfish • Hot Buttered Rum Nectarines
• Rosemary Mustard Pork Tenderloins • Saucy Apricot Chicken
• Herbed Shrimp

110. Family Heirlooms

A celebration of heritage, based on
recipes from past and present

RECIPES 21st-Century Roast Chicken
• Blueberry & Cointreau Bread Pudding • Shepherd's Pie
• Butternut Squash Soup

130. Here Comes the Bride

A nifty little gift box from friends of the bride

RECIPES Cajun Cornish Hens • Pork Chops with Two Mustards

140. Resources: Ways and Means

Tips, tricks and easy techniques, plus
sources to get you started

INTRODUCTION

So What Is This Thing Called Cookbooking?

If you're like me—and like most anybody who loves to cook—you probably have lots of recipes lying around. Some of my recipes used to sit in file boxes (sadly, they were in no particular order); others were crammed into acetate folders; and finally there were the strays, tucked into drawers here and there. As a result, when the time came for a celebration dinner or holiday feast, I had to drop everything and scrounge through dozens of printouts and magazine clips, becoming more aggravated by the minute.

When this happened last Thanksgiving—twelve people, short notice, crammed schedule—I promised myself I'd develop a better system. Thus the concept of Cookbooking was born. It's basically a twist on scrapbooking, with the focus on recipes rather than on photos. It's an ideal way to combine organization with inspiration. Imagine a book of recipes gussied up with menus, pictures, even comments from friends: an album that displays memories of good times as well as the recipes that helped shape them.

If you've scrapbooked before, you'll pick up the notion in a snap; if not, don't worry. Our projects can be managed by even a first-time scrapboooker. Believe me; I'm living proof! Just follow the how-tos and check out the tips and tricks in the last chapter.

On the following pages you'll find a dozen "cookbooks" to spark your imagination. Some are practical and to the point, with few embellishments and extras, such as our binder of quick-to-make suppers. Others are more fanciful and tell a story, like our travel book and heritage album. A few have been expressly developed as gifts, namely our Memory Book and Bride's Recipe Box. But all have one thing in common: They celebrate food in a new, organized and innovative way.

Take a look through our selections; pick your favorites and use them as springboards for your own projects. If you get hungry, not to worry: We've included recipes for each concept to motivate you even more.

Enjoy!

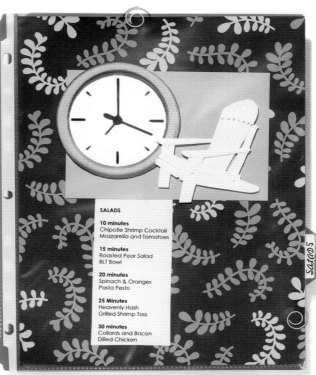

Putting together these books is as much fun as cooking up a great meal.
Try different "ingredients" to give them your own personal touch.

The suitcase cover of this album makes me smile and immediately puts me in another state of mind, triggering many pleasant memories.

On the Road
THE TRAVEL JOURNAL

We all travel for different reasons, but there's probably a single unifying thread: the desire to experience something new, to step out of our everyday lives and into a whole other world.

Over the years, I've been to many far-flung places, from the crowded streets of Beijing to the rugged highlands of Scotland (where you might drive for hours and not spot another person—sheep, yes; people, no). And although I revel in the shopping, the museum-hopping and the journeys down roads less traveled, I remember certain meals with much more clarity than the art at the Louvre or the stained-glass windows at a famous cathedral.

Now don't get me wrong: restaurant-cruising isn't my reason for traveling. But seeking out a variety of places to eat gives me insight into the culture and traditions of a country. I've learned for instance, to avoid restaurants with tourist menus, to opt for the special of the day and to choose a classic dish over something newfangled. I try to order wines from the country of origin, sticking to inexpensive or midpriced ones, and I usually pass on dessert. Checking out what ➤

other people order has proved to be a smart move, and when totally confused, I just put myself in the hands of the waiter. This works especially well in small, casual spots, where the staff might not know any English but they really know the menu.

I'll always remember this lesson from one of my very first trips. My friend Susan and I bravely walked into a small taverna on the island of Crete. The owner took us over to a bin filled with ice and a selection of fresh-caught fish, and after much gesturing, I realized we were each supposed to choose one. But instead, I pointed to the lamb kabobs listed on the blackboard outside. The owner scowled, shook his head and walked away. Recognizing that I had insulted him, I waved him back and reluctantly selected a fish. Clapping his hands and smiling widely, he sat us down, brought us a bottle of wine, a plate of saganaki (fried cheese), two different spreads and a basket of pita bread. While we munched, he went out back to a well-used grill and soon presented me with a filleted trout, perfectly cooked and bursting with the flavors of lemon, rosemary and something else I couldn't quite place (it turned out to be ouzo). A simple salad with chunks of salty feta and homemade almond cake, and that was it. ➤

Bouillabaisse
Pot Au Feu
Coq Au Vin
Tarte Tatin
Quiche Lorraine
Pistou
Tarte Flambe
Crepes
Ratatouille

GET THE LOOK
The Cover

TO DO

● Purchase a 9 1/2" x 11 1/2" post-bound leatherette album.

● Remove posts from album to separate the covers and spine.

● Coat all surfaces with interior/exterior quick-drying spray paint in the color of your choice. (Of course, if you find a color you like, you're good to go, but we were set on a bright red and couldn't find that particular shade.) Let dry.

● Cut eight 2" strips of distressed faux leather, each 9 1/2" x 11 1/2", to fold over the four sides of both back and front covers. With heavy red cotton thread, topstitch along edges of the leather strips on a sewing machine.

● Affix to edges of album with 1/4" double-sided tacky tape.

● Cut 16 triangles from the faux leather to fit corners of covers. (These should measure approximately 4" on the long side of the triangle and 3" on the other two sides.)

● Topstitch with red thread.

● Affix triangles to inside and outside of front and back covers with spray adhesive.

● Cover spine with more faux leather, applied with spray adhesive (no need for topstitching here). Finish off front flap of spine (the piece you see when you open the album) with a topstitched piece of leather. (You could leave the spine as is, but we liked the finished look of the leather.) Affix with spray adhesive.

● Sketch out a handle shape on a piece of plain paper to use as a template. (Our handle is about 1" wide.) Trace shape onto leather four times. Cut out. Topstitch with red thread.

● Trace handle two times on a piece of cardstock. Cut out.

● Sandwich the cardstock between two of the handles, aligning all edges; fasten with glue stick. Repeat to form second handle. Affix to album with glue stick.

It makes you want to pack a bag and take off!
Our suitcase album is proof that you *can*
judge a book by its cover—this journal is stocked
with travel memorabilia,
plus recipes inspired by
the places visited.

*Make straps from two 10 1/2"
lengths of narrow, reversible
ribbon that you run through
tiny brass D-rings. Wrap
around the front cover,
gluing into place on spine
and attaching to back
side of cover with
decorative brads.*

*Embellish cover
with tickets, restaurant
cards, photos, coins or any
other memorabilia from your
trips. Affix pieces with glue stick.
If desired, spell out a foreign phrase
or word such as "bon appétit" or
"mangia" with metal letters
and thread onto ribbon straps.*

No English. No menu. Just simple, sensational food—and a hearty handshake that told me I had done the right thing.

I'll never forget that experience, nor so many other remarkable meals. Sometimes it's the sheer pleasure of food prepared ever so simply with seasonal produce, or concocted with exotic ingredients and a flair for drama; other times it's the environment and the manner of service (I still recall the expectant hush in a Parisian restaurant as the headwaiter sliced into my truffle soufflé); in still other instances, it's the people I've met at a nearby table or the conversation with waiters who want to practice their English. These memories are what motivated me to put together this album, a foodie's answer to a travel diary. The focus is on recipes—either those I've gathered from the cooks I've met or those inspired by my trips. My album doesn't list itineraries or contain lots of photos, but those could be accommodated if you so wish.

Now whenever I search for a recipe, the recollections come flooding back and I take a trip to another place, courtesy of a few pots and pans.

THE INSPIRATION

The first time I went to Europe was more than 30 years ago. It was a vacation to Madrid that my friend Dorothy coordinated, ➤

14

GET THE LOOK
The Dividers

TO DO

- Select heavy 12" x 12" textured papers for your dividers, picking out a different color for each divider. Cut a 4"-wide section off the bottom of each piece of paper, then place over a larger piece, overlapping by about 1" approximately two-thirds of the way down. Topstitch together with a double row of stitches and trim to form a 9" x 11" page. (You can skip this step and simply go with a single sheet of paper, but we preferred the extra detailing.)

- Cut triangles from the distressed leather to affix to the outer corners of all the dividers to mimic the look of the cover. Affix to corners with spray adhesive.

- Topstitch around all three sides of the page, including the triangles and the inner sides of the triangles.
TIP To help the paper move smoothly under the sewing machine, place it atop a piece of waxed paper.

- Affix a band of contrasting paper about one-third of the way down from the top of the page. This will be the border for your title. (See Technique 101 for different border ideas.)

- Spell out the name of your chosen country with metal alphabet tags. Affix to border with tiny brads and glue dots.

- Print a list of favorite dishes on a piece of plain white computer paper. Give the paper an antique look by swiping it over a brown ink pad. (Note: These dishes don't need to correspond to your actual recipes; they're just here to give the "flavor" of the country.)

- Affix list to patterned or solid paper, cut to a slightly larger size, then glue onto page along with a photo, sticker or other ephemera. Add a decorative brad to the top of the list for further adornment.

SPECIAL GEAR
- **Double-sided craft tape:** Terrifically Tacky Tape by Art Accentz ● **Metal alphabet tags and brads:** Art Accentz ● **Textured papers:** Provo Craft

Even these dividers are works of art, thanks to subtle topstitching,
leather corners and recipe listings that make your mouth water.

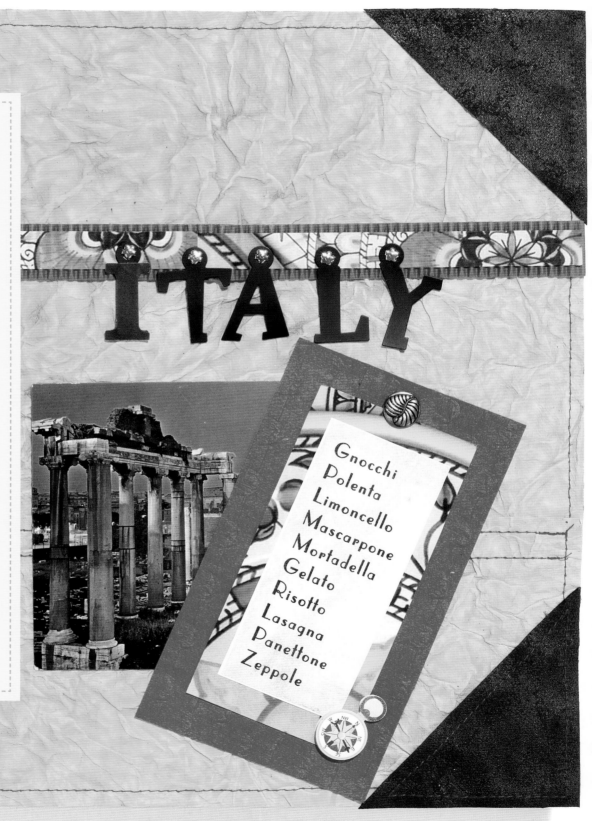

TECHNIQUE 101

Border Line
You can make the title borders for your dividers as simple or fancy as you like, but our guess is that once you get going, you'll want to play around.

1. Fancy: Just cut a strip of fabulously patterned paper about 1" wide and affix to divider page with glue stick. (See France.)

2. Fancier: Cut a boldly patterned strip and affix it atop a slightly wider pleated strip of paper. (See Italy.)

3. Fanciest: Cut about 12 equal-sized squares from different papers (or from one intricately patterned paper) and attach each to a piece of double-sided tape. Peel backing off tape and fasten onto page. (See Spain.)
For other border treatments, see the "Ways and Means" chapter.

ITALY

Gnocchi
Polenta
Limoncello
Mascarpone
Mortadella
Gelato
Risotto
Lasagna
Panettone
Zeppole

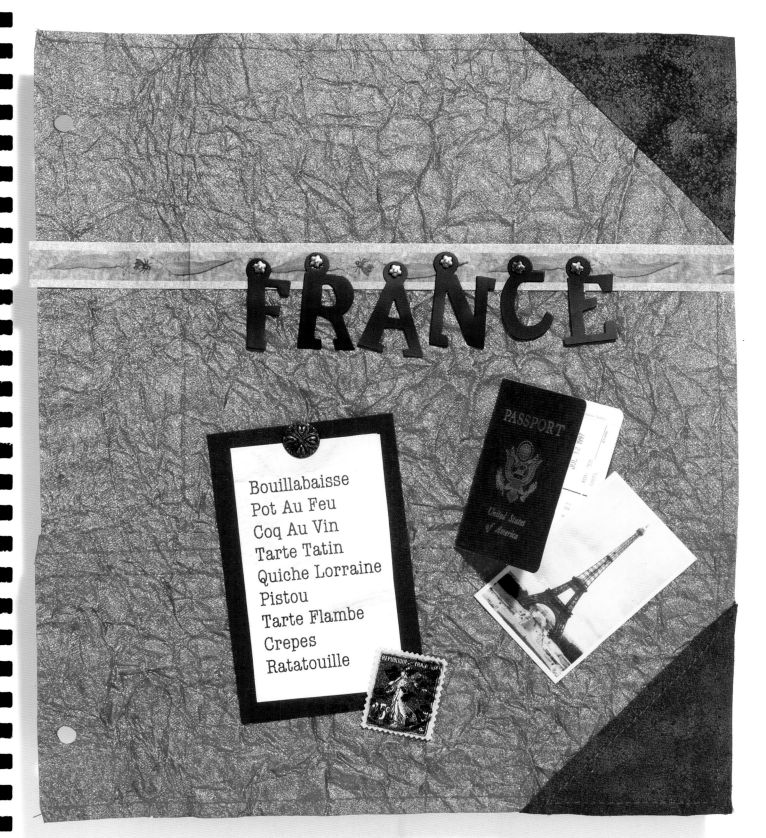

FRANCE

Bouillabaisse
Pot Au Feu
Coq Au Vin
Tarte Tatin
Quiche Lorraine
Pistou
Tarte Flambe
Crepes
Ratatouille

a deal she fell into that we couldn't refuse. To this day I can see us walking through the dark and dusty corridors of the Prado (it's been renovated since then), oohing and aahing over the huge canvases. And then there was the bus trip to Toledo, where we viewed awesome paintings by El Greco, among other wonders. But one of my favorite recollections is an incredible paella dinner we shared with two handsome Spanish guys who were buddies of a college friend.

We ordered two different kinds of paella: Valenciana (made with chicken and seafood) and Mariscos (seafood only), and neither was like anything I'd ever eaten in New York's estimable Spanish restaurants. At that dinner I learned that part of the secret of paella was flavoring the broth with shrimp shells and cooking the rice in such a way that some of it gets toasted.

I came home and signed up for a Spanish cooking class almost immediately. And I am pleased to say, I can now whip up a fantastic paella, along with garlic soup and a lovely flan.

Even though I didn't realize it at the time, that original venture was a clue to my travel style. I not only like trying new cuisines, I like experimenting with them when I return. Although I'm ➤

GET THE LOOK
The Pages

TO DO

● Cut brown kraft paper to size and crumple. Place a tea cloth over the paper and iron gently.

● Affix photos, menus, tickets, etc., to the kraft paper pages with a glue stick.

● Adorn some of the pages with an alphabet stamp, spelling out names of cities, dishes or other relevant terms. Add more words with self-sticking bubble letters.

● Use a tag punch to punch out small sections from maps; affix to pages with small star brads.

● Print out or write recipes on parchment cardstock.

Not just vehicles for recipes, the pages also display mementos from trips.

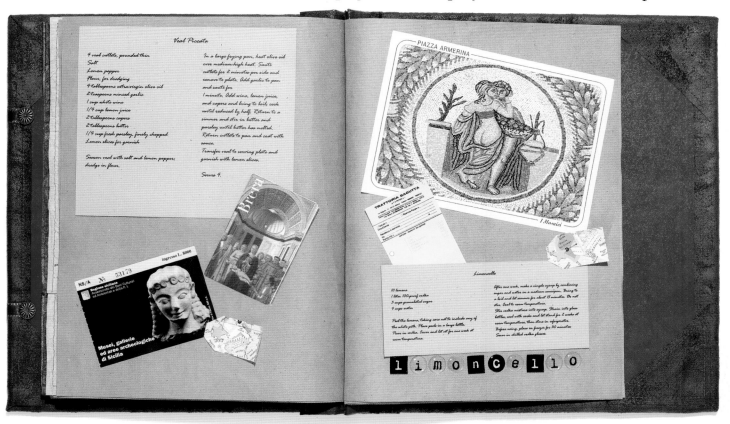

notoriously bad about keeping records of where I've been or what I've seen, I always manage to bring back a jumble of restaurant cards, matchbooks, menus and notes scribbled on napkins. So, along with my stockpile of memories, this paraphernalia was the fuel for my *Cookbooking* project, along with a vague idea for making the journal resemble a suitcase. And that's where designer Pattie Donham came in.

The suitcase cover of this album makes me smile and immediately puts me in another state of mind, triggering pleasant thoughts of times away. The only danger is that I'll start daydreaming as I turn the pages and forget to watch the pot on the stove! I also adore the dividers with leather corners that echo the cover. And Pattie outdid herself with the little map tags. She cut them out with a tag punch from huge maps I gave her, zeroing in on specific locations.

Now that I'm back from a recent trip to Paris, I'm ready to start adding more pages—once I decipher my notes about spicy shrimp on mustard polenta and figure out how to make black chocolate fondant (yum!). ■ ■ ■

GET THE LOOK
Finishing Touches

Rather than complicate the cover with a title, we stitched up a matching luggage tag and hung it from the handle—a clever 3-D element that emphasizes the theme. You can also substitute a store-bought tag.

TO DO

- Cut out two matching rectangles from the faux leather and snip out a rectangular opening in the center of one.

- Cut out a piece of acetate the same size and place between the leather rectangles.

- Topstitch though leather and plastic on three sides with red thread. Make a name tag from the parchment cardstock, fill in and slip under the acetate.

- Punch hole through tag, slip through a small chain and attach to handle.

DIFFERENT TAKES

Rather than using textured paper for the dividers, make color copies of maps of the appropriate countries and embellish each with the country's name in a letter format of your choice.

For a simpler cover, forgo the cards, tickets and so on and keep the surface clean, with just the straps and luggage tag as embellishments.

Instead of kraft paper for the backgrounds, color-key the pages to your dividers with a selection of scrapbook papers.

Recipes to Try

Classic Gazpacho

Serves 8

● Often called "liquid salad," gazpacho has many variations. Although there are lots of ingredients, it's a cinch to make because you basically just chop up the vegetables and puree. This also makes a nice sauce for a cold pasta salad; just toss with cooked ziti or penne and garnish with shredded fresh basil.

6 ripe tomatoes, peeled and chopped

1 red onion, finely chopped

1 cucumber, peeled, seeded and chopped

1 sweet red (or green) bell pepper, seeded and chopped

2 stalks celery, chopped

1–2 tablespoons fresh parsley, chopped

2 tablespoons fresh basil, chopped

2 tablespoons fresh chives, chopped, plus 2 tablespoons more for garnish

3 cloves garlic, minced

¼ cup red wine vinegar

¼ cup olive oil

2 tablespoons freshly squeezed lemon juice

4 cups tomato juice

2 teaspoons sugar

Kosher salt and fresh ground pepper to taste

6 or more drops of Tabasco sauce to taste

1 teaspoon Worcestershire sauce

Combine all ingredients in a blender, starting with only 1 cup of the tomato juice. Pulse to a chunky consistency. Add the rest of the tomato juice and blend. Cover and refrigerate overnight. Garnish with the reserved chopped chives.

Note: For an even heftier gazpacho, use less tomato juice.

Sometimes the simplest dishes are the best, releasing fresh, pure flavors that satisfy hunger and delight the palate.

Mussels with White Wine, Butter and Garlic

Serves 6

4 lbs. mussels, rinsed and scrubbed well under cold running water

2 cups dry white wine

4 shallots, very finely chopped

4 garlic cloves, peeled and very finely chopped

⅓ teaspoon salt

⅓ teaspoon ground pepper

⅓ cup mixed fresh green herbs, chopped (parsley, basil, tarragon but almost any kind will do)

6 tablespoons butter, cut into pieces

Rinse and scrub the mussels well under cold running water. Remove the beards from shells and discard.

Combine wine, shallots, garlic and salt in a large stockpot and simmer for 5 minutes.

Add the mussels. Cover the pot and increase heat to high.

Cook about 5 minutes or until all the mussels have opened.

Stir in the herbs and butter and remove from heat.

Divide the mussels among four soup bowls. Pour broth over the mussels and serve with some crusty bread for sopping up the sauce.

The charm of this book begins with its whimsical cover, fabric-printed, with a 1950s kitchen scene, complete with smiling women in aprons.

Down Memory Lane

THE MEMORY COOKBOOK

Some of our strongest memories are triggered by food. The smell of bacon frying can conjure up lazy Sunday breakfasts; the creaminess of mac-n-cheese can summon the comforts of childhood. The experience of cooking, eating and sharing meals is a powerful force that stimulates a chain of recollections.

I know I can never look at an artichoke and not think of Dennis K., a one-time boyfriend who took me to a very special, very expensive restaurant only to lose his cool when he couldn't figure out how to eat his steamed artichoke with lemon-garlic sauce. And to this day I channel my friend Lindsay whenever I prepare a soufflé. It was our come-on-over dinner standby during our first years of working in Manhattan, made with cheap cheese and served with even cheaper wine. Although I've since mastered crab-and-Grand Marnier soufflés, my mind always replays those simple suppers with friends.

So when Pattie Donham, the imaginative crafter behind PattiWack designs, told me about a recipe/memory album she made for her mother, a light bulb went on over my head. What a fabulous *Cookbooking* idea! ➤

Like Pattie, you can create a keepsake based on a loved one's recipes, tucking in reminiscences and photos from family and friends. Or you could turn things around and gather recipes from others that the recipient might want to try. Or, easiest of all, you could "cookbook" some recipes from your own files as a gift for that friend who's always saying, "I love this. Can you give me the recipe?" How you tweak the concept is up to you.

THE INSPIRATION

When Pattie created her album for her mother Pearl's 70th birthday, the original goal was a straightforward collection of memoirs and photographs. "I asked everyone in the family to write something down about my mom—a letter, a poem, a story, whatever they wanted—and more than half the time their recollections involved food," Pattie says.

This got Pattie thinking. Why not go a step further and include Pearl's own famed recipes in the book—all the favorites everyone talked about? "Now my mom has a cookbook plus a memory book. She can flip through the pages and know that wherever we are in the world, we love her kitchen best."

The new concept not only resulted in a more unique album, but also made perfect sense because Pearl was always in the kitchen. As the wife of a Pentecostal preacher ➤

The Cover

TO DO

● Cut two pieces of foamcore approximately 10" x 12 ¼" and glue cotton batting onto top surfaces.

● Cut two pieces of fabric, each 2" larger all around than the foamcore. Wrap over the foamcore and batting, pulling tightly into place, and affix to back of foamcore with spray adhesive.

● Cut two pieces of textured paper just a bit smaller than the foamcore, and with spray adhesive, affix onto the back sides of the covers to hide the glued-on fabric.
TIP Spray entire piece of paper with the adhesive, then immediately attach.

● Next, with a grommet kit, insert three large grommets on the left edge of front cover; repeat on the right edge of back cover.

"I wanted something very colorful, very retro, and this fabric was exactly right," says Pattie. "It reminds me of my mom, who to this day welcomes me home with a hug and a pie."

SPECIAL GEAR
● **Sticker letters:** Stickopatomus by EK Success or Alphabitties by Provocraft
● **Chef's hat** (on cover): EK Success
● **Fabric for cover:** available at cheap-threads.com

Embellish front cover by affixing a tiny chef's hat embrodidered with the words "Kiss the Cook."

To "wrap up" the album, cut a length of ribbon 48" long and affix to center of inside back cover before you glue on the textured paper. Bring around to front and tie a bow.

in the Midwest, she was constantly cooking up a storm—making meals for church suppers and baking cakes and pies for sales.

On top of all this, she had three kids and a husband to feed. "Even when money was tight, my mother managed to put a delicious meal on the table and whip up a special dessert," Pattie recalls. "I was a problem because I was a picky eater and would rather have lettuce than anything else. So Mom came up with a salad that included broccoli, bacon, raisins and sunflower seeds to pack some nutrition into me. It's still something I eat all the time, and it's the recipe I included in my section of the book."

As for Pearl, she didn't get to look at the book until after her birthday party. "Someone grabbed it out of my hands and that was that," she says. Guests passed it around, pausing at different pages and trading tales of their own. One story sparked another as the letters and recipes transported people to times gone by. "I didn't understand what all the fuss was until the following day, when I sat down with some tea and started reading. Then the memories came flooding back," Pearl states. "Pattie did a real good job putting this together, even if she still doesn't eat enough." ■ ■ ■

GET THE LOOK
The Pages

TO DO

● Start by collecting, then printing out people's memoirs on the computer, using different fonts to give personality to each remembrance. Trim the edges of these printouts with decorative scissors or adorn with ribbons, stickers or hand-drawn borders.

● Gather recipes: These can also be computer-printed, or can be handwritten on index cards or notebook paper.

● Collect photos. Add mats or borders, if desired.

● Select embellishments: charms, stickers, borders, sticker letters, etc., and add to pages as desired.

● Glue photos, memoirs and recipes onto 8 ½" x 11" scrapbook papers, both patterned and solid.

● Trim the left edges of 8 ½" x 11" top-loading page protectors for a cleaner, less hard-edged look.

● Organize papers according to contributor and slip into protectors. Then use a three-hole punch to cut holes in the protectors and the scrapbook papers.

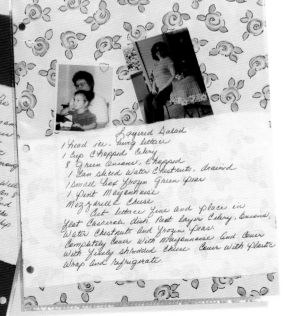

I LOVE YOU NANNY

Tricia

Nanny, you are so Strong...
You continue to assure me that I can do whatever I put my mind to.
With you in my life I have always felt strong enough to conquer all situations. – (Some just took longer than others. Sorry about that!) me.

Nanny, you are so Forgiving...
Out of everyone and anyone- You have never turned your back on me.
You teach our family that "time heals all wounds".

Nanny, you are so Helpful...
You are always willing to do anything to help the ones you love.
Helped me collect Barbies each and every year.

Nanny, you are so Creative...
Helped me to see that some people's trash can be our treasures.
When I did not have much money you made me everything for Lacricia's baby room.

Nanny, you are so Memorable...
I remember having fun, lying on a mattress in the backyard watching the stars.
Taught me how fun "people watching" can be.

Nanny, you are so Loving...
I feel like you are a part of me – Like my other half.
You always remember everyone's birthdays like clockwork.

Nanny, you are so YOU...
There is no other person in this world like you.
Thank you for never changing and always being true to yourself!

Happy 70th Birthday!
Forever and Always...I Love You Soooooooo Much!
Tricia LeAnn

FOUR GENERATIONS

Open the book
and you are treated
to glimpses
of Pearl's life, as
told in the words
of her family.

Mike's Lemon Pie

1¼ cups sugar
6 tbsp cornstarch
2 cups Water
⅓ cups fresh lemon juice

3 egg yolks
3 tbsp butter
1½ tsp lemon extract
2 tsp. vinegar

Mix sugar and cornstarch together in heavy sauce pan; Add Water. Combine egg yolks and lemon juice And add to mixture. Cook until thick stirring Constantly. Add lemon extract And vinegar And Stir Weel. The vinegar does Away With the starchy taste. Pour into baked pie shell and top with Meringue. Brown in Oven.

BEAUTIFUL

Tricia's Corn Dip

3 small Cans shoe-peg Corn
16 oz. sour Cream
16 oz. Mayonnaise
3 fresh Jalapeno Peppers (diced fine)
3 Green Onions, Chopped fine
Mix together And chill. Serve With Chips and Crackers.

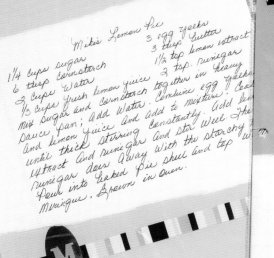

Aboard

Pattie

Broccoli Salad

1 bunch Broccoli (broken into small pieces)
½ cup finely Chopped red Onion
1 cup finely Chopped Celery
1 lb. bacon, fried Crisp And Crumbled
½ cup Sunflower Seeds
½ cup Raisins
Mix together And Add Dressing Just before serving.
        Dressing: ¾ cup Mayonnaise
                  ¼ cup Sugar
                  2 tbsp Cider Vinegar

WHERE HAS THE TIME GONE

DIFFERENT TAKES

For another cover look, create a photo collage of all the people who have contributed to the album. You could also have the photos screened onto fabric, then proceed as Pattie did with her 1950s fabric cover. Another idea is to use a single photo of the recipient.

Wrap the rings with yarn or braid for a more streamlined look. Or, go more retro by attaching charms or buttons or beads. You could also forget the rings entirely and bind the pages together with raffia or twine. (Note: This works better for an album with fewer pages, because raffia is not as sturdy as a metal ring.)

Include a brief profile of each contributor on the divider pages, with name, occupation, residence, relationship to recipient and other pertinent information.

Nanny

Sister

Pearl

Honey

Tootsie

Family

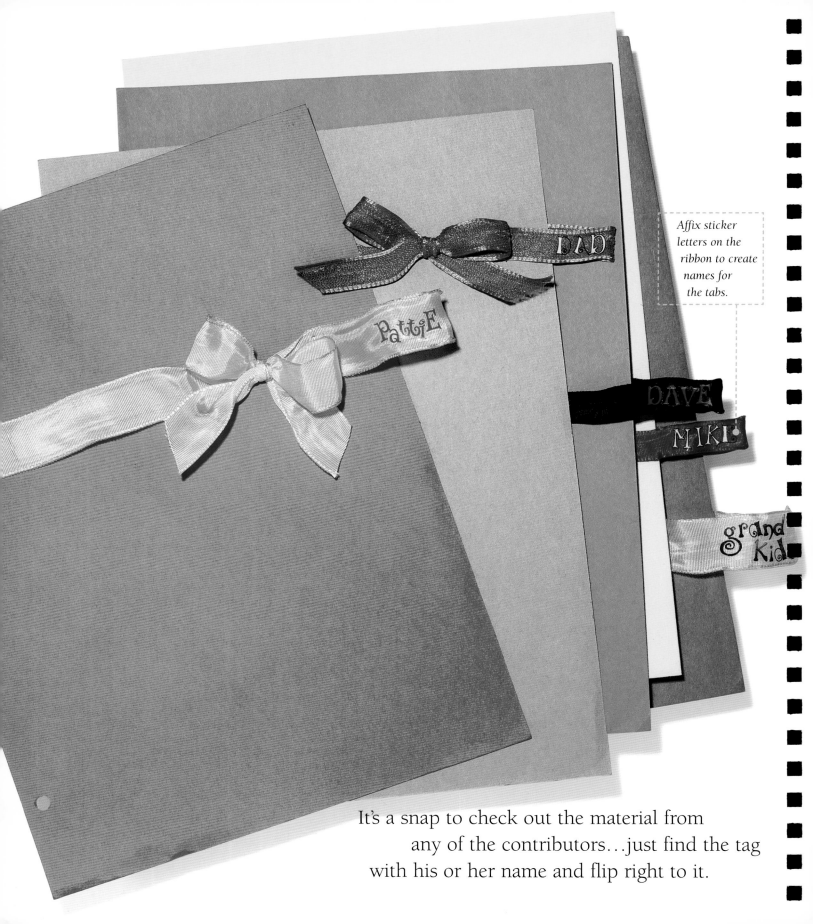

*Affix sticker
letters on the
ribbon to create
names for
the tabs.*

DAD

Pattie

DAVE

MIKE

grand
Kid

It's a snap to check out the material from
any of the contributors…just find the tag
with his or her name and flip right to it.

The Dividers

TO DO

Colorful ribbon dividers separate the album into sections devoted to different family members. This savvy spin on the usual index tabs gives the book a down-home touch.

- Take 9" x 12" pieces of construction paper in different colors, match up the holes with those on scrapbook papers and use a three-hole punch to cut holes.

- Cut a length of ribbon approximately 25" long and glue it horizontally along construction paper, tying in a bow toward outer edge. Make sure to extend ribbon an inch or so beyond paper's edge (this is the part that will be the "tab") and wrap ribbon around to back of paper, affixing with tacky glue.

- As you're making the dividers, remember to stagger the ribbons, putting the ribbon on first divider near the top of the paper and positioning the rest further down on the pages so the ribbon tabs don't cover each other.

- Slip the dividers into the appropriate places between the pages.

Finishing Touches

TO DO

- Double-check the order of the pages and stack together.

- Thread the three 2 ½" metal rings through grommets to hold pages together.

- Embellish the rings with 6" strips of ribbon in different colors and patterns. About twenty strips should do the trick; just knot around the ring until covered.

The beribboned binder rings give the book a frilly flourish that's a cinch to accomplish. "Plain rings just look too industrial," Pattie notes.

31

Recipes to Try

Pearl's recipes are deliciously down-home, which explains why everyone loves her cooking.

Broccoli Salad

Serves 2 as a main dish

● This is what Pattie grew up on and still loves.

For the salad:

1 bunch broccoli, cut up into small pieces

$^1/_2$ cup red onion, finely chopped

1 cup celery, finely chopped

1 lb. bacon, fried and crumbled

$^1/_2$ cup sunflower seeds

$^1/_2$ cup raisins

For the mayonnaise dressing:

$^3/_4$ cup mayonnaise

$^1/_4$ cup sugar

2 tablespoons cider vinegar

Fold dressing ingredients together until well blended. Refrigerate until ready to use.

Into 2-quart saucepan of boiling water, place broccoli. Boil for 1 minute; immediately plunge broccoli into cold water to stop cooking and retain color. Dry thoroughly.

Combine salad ingredients in large bowl. Add dressing just before serving.

Sour Cream Raisin Pie

Serves 6–8

● Pearl's easy-make pie has always been a top pick at church socials.

For the filling:

1 cup sour cream

1 cup sugar

2 eggs

1 cup raisins

$^1/_2$ teaspoon cinnamon

1 scant pinch ground cloves

$^1/_4$ teaspoon salt

1 tablespoon butter, softened

For the crust:

One 9" frozen pie shell, thawed and baked according to package instructions.

For the pie base:

1 package softened cream cheese

$^1/_2$ cup confectioner's sugar

3 cups whipped topping

Make the filling: In a medium saucepan, combine all filling ingredients, mixing well to blend. Cook over medium heat, stirring until thick (about 10 minutes). Chill thoroughly.

Make the pie base: Mix the cream cheese and sugar until well blended. Take $^2/_3$ of mixture and spread over bottom of baked piecrust.

Pour pie filling over pie base mixture and spread evenly.

Take the remaining pie base mixture and gently blend with the whipped topping. Top pie with this and refrigerate. Serve cold or at room temperature.

The Littlest Chefs
A KID'S COOKBOX

As a kid, I loved cooking with my parents. It made me feel like such an adult. And it was much more fun than helping to wash the dishes!

I remember making Toll House cookies, Rice Krispie treats and sour cream Bundt cake after school with my mother. Of course, the best part was licking the bowl (and in the case of the Rice Krispie treats, finishing off the bag of marshmallows). But sweets weren't the only thing we collaborated on. She taught me to make a mean marinara sauce as well as pork chops Provençal (a dish I still serve). My dad did his part, too, teaching me the art of hamburger cookery. I'd help mix the ground beef with different herbs and a dash of red pepper flakes, then watch as he carefully seared the patties in a skillet, flipping them over at just the right second.

I'll never forget the day when, at age 7, I got carried away and tossed in too many of those red pepper flakes. Just one bite and we all started coughing and I thought I'd never be allowed to cook again. But my father, God bless him, gave me a hug and simply commented, "Well, even the best cooks goof up sometimes."

I credit those occasions with the fact that I enjoy cooking so much, and I'm thrilled when I see ➤

parents creating meals with their kids. With childhood obesity at an all-time high, teaching children about nutrition and food prep is imperative—and the best way to do that is right at home. Which is why we've come up with something out of the box—literally. It's a see-through lunchbox, crammed with kid-friendly recipes indexed with funky foam letters. There's also a booklet for Mom on how to prepare healthy meals.

THE INSPIRATION

Curious to see if my instincts were on target, I showed the box to Lori, the 8-year-old daughter of a friend in my apartment building. Lori is a real New York City kid, as comfortable dining at gourmet restaurants as standing on line at McDonald's. She can order a hamburger "medium rare and no salt please" as easily as veal piccata, and is the only child I know who actually likes escargots. She also ➤

The Cover

TO DO

- Cut a sheet of 12" x 12" craft foam in half.
- Draw letters of child's name using a stencil as your guide.
- Cut out letters with a swivel knife.
- Affix with glue dots or special foam glue.
- Adorn with self-adhesive buttons or a foam doll or animal. You can also use stickers, charms or ribbons for embellishments.

SPECIAL GEAR
- **Lunchbox:** clear boxes in different sizes are available at thecontainerstore.com
- **Self-adhesive buttons:** EK Success
- **Foam letters, shapes and sheets:** Fibre-Craft
- **Fastenator stapler and decorative staples:** EK Success

The best thing about this project is its simplicity. It's mostly a matter of cutting and pasting. You can sit down and finish the whole caboodle in just an evening or spend an afternoon putting it together with a child.

Not really a cover at all but a name card, this piece of craft foam sits right inside the front of the CookBox, declaring its owner to all who look. The box itself is a clear 12" x 6" lunchbox—easy to clean and easy to decorate if so desired.

spends time cooking with her teenage sister, whose goal is to be the next Martha Stewart.

So I waited expectantly as Lori checked out the box. Her first words were "Why didn't you put my name on it?" Then she announced, "The whisk is too little. I use a regular one."

Despite the size of the whisk, I knew we'd scored a hit here, and I'd like to pass along a few tips I've learned about cooking with kids, some courtesy of Lori herself:

1. Encourage kids to cook by teaching them to bake. Baking offers them the opportunity to mix and sift (something even little boys like to do), and the ingredients are child-friendly—the items smell good, taste good and are reassuringly familiar. Cutting out cookie shapes, assembling a cake and shaping a piecrust are techniques small fry can manage, and they'll pave the way for other cooking scenarios. ➤

GET THE LOOK
The Dividers

TO DO

- Select sheets of craft foam in the colors of your choice and cut to fit box (ours measure approximately 12" x 6").

- Affix self-adhesive foam letters to top edge of each sheet to spell out category labels (breakfast, lunch, dinner, etc.). Remember to stagger the labels from left to right so that at least part of each can be seen when stacked in the box.

- Outline index tab shape around letters with a pencil; trim to size.

Made of the same soft, pliable craft foam as the name card, the dividers are a playful riff on ordinary construction paper or poster board.

BREAKFAST

Affix foam animal shapes and googly eyes with glue dots.

DINNER

LUNCH

37

2. Zero in on your child's favorite dishes and cook them together. Use the time shared to explain the history or culture behind the dish as well as to practice cooking skills. Once they've mastered a recipe, show them variations and allow them to try their own concoctions.

3. Get kids involved with the science of measuring. Buy them their own set of colorful measuring cups and spoons and have them help when you're making dinner. It will acquaint them with proportion and scale and instill a sense of confidence. Even tasks like getting the right amount of butter can be a mini-math lesson. For instance, if a recipe calls for 4 tablespoons of butter and an entire stick is 8 tablespoons, ask your child to figure out the correct amount.

4. Let kids pitch in with all the steps of making a recipe, from food prep to cleanup. Include tasks like washing the salad greens, putting ingredients away, setting the table and stashing the leftovers. This will familiarize them with following a project through from beginning to end.

5. Entice even the most disinterested child by making meatballs. Both very small and older ➤

GET THE LOOK
The Pages

TO DO

● Cut pieces of construction paper in different colors a little shorter than the dividers (ours are 12" x 5").

● **For flat pages:** Print out recipes, pictures and titles and cut the printouts into several different pieces—ingredients on one, title on another, instructions on a third. Arrange printouts as desired on construction paper and affix with a glue stick. Make holes with a single-hole punch near the top edges of some of the pages. String different colored ribbons through holes and tie into bows.

● **For flap pages:** Prepare recipes as above, affixing to construction paper. Cut a smaller piece of coordinating construction paper, about 6" x 4", to cover part of recipe. Place near left edge and affix with glue stick. Fold back about an inch from edge to form a flap. Embellish flap with self-adhesive buttons and Fastenator staples along with a photo of the recipe or any doodles your child may want to add.

● **For Mom's booklet:** Print out (or cut out) tips and advice on healthy eating. Affix to matching pieces of construction paper with glue stick. Embellish with self-adhesive buttons. Attach pages together with a Fastenator (a decorative stapler that features soft staple bands in different colors). Place a piece of ribbon under center staple for extra adornment.

TIP As an alternative, you might attach pages together with scrapbooking brads or "weave" them together by punching holes and threading a ribbon through the pages. A regular stapler is also fine.

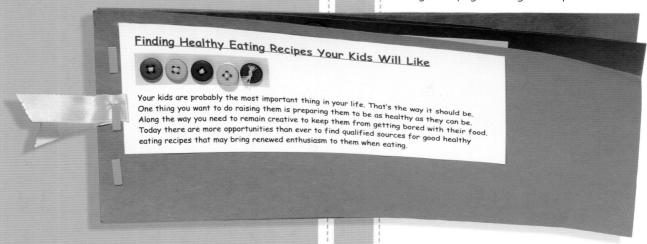

Finding Healthy Eating Recipes Your Kids Will Like

Your kids are probably the most important thing in your life. That's the way it should be. One thing you want to do raising them is preparing them to be as healthy as they can be. Along the way you need to remain creative to keep them from getting bored with their food. Today there are more opportunities than ever to find qualified sources for good healthy eating recipes that may bring renewed enthusiasm to them when eating.

Jam Pennies

12 slices of white or brown bread
2 Tbsp. butter, softened
6 oz. strawberry jam

Preparation:
Cut the crusts from bread, then lightly spread each slice with butter. Spread six slices with jam, and then sanwich them together with the remaining buttered bread.
Using a round pastry cutter, stamp out four circles from each sandwich. Arrange on a serving plate and serve as soon as possible.

Bigger and better than index cards, these recipes are fun to look at, emblazoned with sprightly lettering and appetizing pictures. Some have clever peekaboo flaps to invite further viewing.

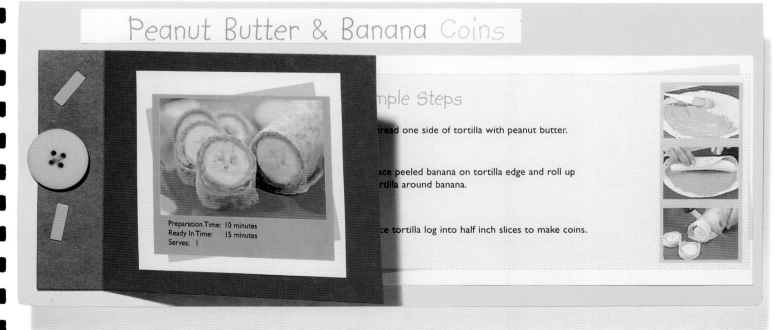

Peanut Butter & Banana Coins

...mple Steps

...read one side of tortilla with peanut butter.

...ace peeled banana on tortilla edge and roll up ...rtilla around banana.

...ce tortilla log into half inch slices to make coins.

Preparation Time: 10 minutes
Ready In Time: 15 minutes
Serves: 1

children love mixing up the ground meat, herbs and bread crumbs with their hands and shaping the mixture into balls. It's almost like working with Play-Doh! Use your own recipe and let 'em rock.

Once you've introduced your children to the pleasures of cooking, spur them on further with our innovative CookBox. Create it on your own and give it as a surprise that you can use together. Or, if you like to craft with your kids, make it a rainy-afternoon collaboration (see ideas in "Different Takes").

Either way, the CookBox will open up all sorts of cooking adventures. ■ ■ ■

Ribbons, charms, beads, toys—kids love the little extras that make an item special. Our CookBox sports a kicky bunch of bows and a funny foam doll.

Finishing Touches

TO DO

● Attach a kid-sized utensil, such as a whisk or wooden spoon, and a foam doll or animal to the handle of box, then tie on several different ribbons.

DIFFERENT TAKES

Decorate the box itself with stickers, charms, even paint. We left ours clear so it could be repurposed for something else, but it's ideal for gussying up. Ditto for the cards themselves. Encourage your child to add his or her own drawings, comments or any other adornment.

Amp up the name card with a photo of the child. Just attach with a glue stick. Or, instead of a photo, your child can draw a self-portrait on construction paper.

For a less frilly look, replace the ribbons on the cards and the handles with shoelaces, pipe cleaners, raffia or strands of leather. Again, let your child do the choosing.

Instead of printing out recipes, let your children write out a few of his or her favorites on colorful index cards. Cut to size and glue onto the construction paper.

Recipes to Try

Frozen Fruity Yogurt Pops

Serves 4

● Even little kids can manage this recipe. Bonus: This treat is healthy as well as delicious.

One 8-ounce container of berry-flavored yogurt

$\frac{1}{2}$ cup fresh berries (if using strawberries, they should be chopped into smaller pieces)

4 small paper cups

Wooden craft sticks

Pour the yogurt into the cups, dividing equally so that each cup contains the same amount.

Stir in berries, leaving some room near tops of the cups.

Stretch plastic wrap over each cup.

With a craft stick, make a hole in the middle of the plastic wrap and insert stick into cup so it stands up straight.

Put cups in freezer until yogurt is frozen solid.

Unwrap plastic, peel off cup and enjoy.

The CookBox will open up all sorts of cooking adventures.

Peewee Pizza

Serves 1

● As a child, I used to make these all the time, popping the muffins into the toaster oven for even easier cooking. Once I learned the basics, I would rev up my pizzas by adding mushrooms, olives, diced peppers or whatever topping was my favorite pick-of-the-moment.

1 English muffin

4 tablespoons jarred marinara sauce

Dried oregano

Dried basil

Red pepper flakes

Freshly ground black pepper

8–10 strips mozzarella cheese (about 2 inches long, $\frac{1}{3}$ inch wide)

6 pepperoni slices

Grated Parmesan cheese

Separate English muffin into halves.

Stir a pinch of oregano, basil and red pepper flakes into the sauce. Add freshly ground pepper.

Spread sauce on top of English muffin, adding extra if you want a "saucier" pizza.

Place slices of mozzarella on top.

Place three pepperoni slices on each muffin half.

Sprinkle grated Parmesan cheese over each half.

Put on a baking sheet and heat in a low oven (250 degrees F) for 5–8 minutes, or until cheese is slightly melted.

I - COOK

FAST
EASY
QUICK
SIMPLE

This *"look at me"* cover is basically a cut-and-paste job,
made up of different papers and some adhesive letters.

Where's Dinner?

THE SIMPLE SUPPERS BOOK

Back when I was the executive editor of *Family Circle* magazine, a publication that prints lots and lots of food pages, I learned two things about cooking that stuck in my mind:

1. The majority of Americans rely on only about ten recipes and make them again and again, year after year.

2. Anything longer than half an hour is too long when it comes to preparing dinner.

So much for turning to anything in Julia Child's *Mastering the Art of French Cooking*. But the stats do make sense. Tried-and-true recipes are a security blanket: You know they work, and no one will be disappointed. As for the thirty minutes, when your family is hungry, even half an hour seems like forever. Although *Family Circle* readers did request new and different dishes, they didn't want anything "too different." And while they were willing to spend more time and effort on weekend dinners or special occasions, when it came to schooldays and workdays—no way. Thanks to a brilliant food department, we managed to give readers what they wanted and came up with some strategies that might work for you, too:

1. Take a favorite recipe and give it a twist. ➤

SALADS

10 minutes
Chipotle Shrimp Cock[...]
Mozzarella and Tomat[...]

15 minutes
Roasted Pear Salad
BLT Bowl

20 minutes
Spinach & Oranges
Pasta Pesto

25 Minutes
Heavenly Hash
Grilled Shrimp Toss

30 minutes
Collards and Bacon
Dilled Chicken

ENTREES

10 minutes
Herbed Tuna
Curried Tilapia

15 minutes
Orange Roughy
Beef Stir-Fry

20 minutes
Mexican Ceviche
Pasta Salad

25 minutes
Shrimp Curry
6-can Chili

30 minutes
Eggplant Parmagiana
Turkey Enchilada

SiMple suppers

Look to those recipes you make again and again and attempt new versions. Chili, for instance, has an infinite number of variations: Make it with beef; try it with turkey; keep it vegetarian. Top it with cornbread or stuff it into poblano peppers. You can even spike it with tequila, a trick my friend Trish swears by (and she's hosted many a successful chili party).

2. Expand on a favorite cuisine. If your family loves Italian food, introduce other dishes to your repertoire. Start with pasta—always a favorite—and bring on new shapes and sauces such as limone, made with fresh lemon juice. Move from veal piccata to veal saltimbocca (veal scallopini rolled around sage leaves and prosciutto), switch from chicken parmigiana to chicken florentine (similar, but with the addition of spinach). To get started, check out tuscanytonight.com and italianchef.com as well as general sites such as epicurious.com and foodnetwork.com.

3. Think "make-ahead." Many recipes have steps that can be done in advance. In fact, restaurant chefs do this all the time. Make a sauce one day and chill it for use later on in the week; do all your chopping the evening before. Even if a recipe doesn't specify "make-ahead," there's usually something you can prep beforehand to shave time off the cooking process.

4. Rely on quick-cooking ingredients. Couscous is a gift from heaven, ready in just a little more time than it takes to boil water. ➤

GET THE LOOK
The Cover

TO DO

● Start with a vinyl loose-leaf binder, one with a clear plastic sleeve over both front and back covers. Ours measures 11 ½" x 11 ½", but any size will do; just trim your papers to fit.

● Select two coordinating 12" x 12" patterned papers for the front cover, one for the "border" (we chose a brown and green floral) and one for the background (ours is striped). Cut the background paper 7 ½" wide and paste over the other one with a glue stick to achieve a border/background effect. Trim to an 11" x 11" size to fit the binder.

● Next, select two solid papers to form the title panel. Cut the bottom one (ours is brown) into an 11" x 3 ½" rectangle; cut the other ¼" smaller all around. Shape this with a corner punch. Center the smaller piece on the larger one and affix with glue stick.

● Glue title panel onto cover papers about 1 ½" down from top edge.

● Sketch or download and print an image of a clock face and affix it below title panel. (Print out at least six of these images to use throughout your book.)

● Affix more alphabet stickers, smaller this time, to spell out words "fast," "easy," "quick," "simple," or whatever you desire.

● Slip cover page into the plastic binder sleeve.

● For back cover, simply cut another paper to size and slip into sleeve.

● If inside front cover has pockets, add more papers cut to size. Use this area for tucking in loose recipes and cards.

The key to this book is its gorgeous papers,
so take some time to select a group that
mixes and matches well.

Spell out title with alphabet stickers. We liked the idea of "i-cook," but this could be anything you want.

I - COOK

FAST
EASY
QUICK
SIMPLE

A store-bought binder with plastic sleeves makes this project a snap to create.

You can gussy it up in all sorts of ways, adding raisins, nuts or sun-dried tomatoes; or simply buy a packaged couscous mix that comes with its own seasoning. Polenta, made from cornmeal, is another standby available in ready-made, easy-to-slice rolls. You just cut off a few chunky slices, sauté or grill them, and top them with cheese and herbs or a chunky tomato sauce. And chicken cutlets are the best thing since sliced bread. They cook up in no time and marry well with countless ingredients. One of my no-fail tricks is to put them in a baking dish, season with herbes de Provence and douse with a creamy salad dressing. Add diced sun-dried tomatoes, capers and maybe some olives. Pop in a 350-degree oven and bake until golden.

5. An additional strategy: Gather all your recipes and devote an evening to cookbooking. The concept we have in mind is a simple binder you jazz up with a series of gorgeous papers. A little gluing here and there and some punch lists of quick-fix dishes, and dinner just got a whole lot easier.

THE INSPIRATION

Since the theme of this book is simple suppers, the book itself called for a simple approach. That meant a loose-leaf binder, something anyone can pick up at a stationery or craft store. The key to success? Absolutely fabulous papers. ➤

GET THE LOOK
The Dividers

TO DO

● Select different patterned scrapbook papers for each divider; cut to 8 1/2" x 11".

● Cut a 6" x 4" panel from coordinating solid-colored pieces of paper.

● Glue clock image and whimsical sticker to panel with glue stick. (We decided not to be at all literal here and used images like a porch rocker, a ballet tutu and a pair of boots, but you could do food icons as well.)

● Select your favorite recipes in each category and make computer printouts with the recipe names and the time they require on plain white paper. This is your "punch list" of quick, reliable dishes. Slip under title panel and affix everything to scrapbook paper with a glue stick. Slip page into clear plastic sleeve.

● Print index tab titles for the various categories and affix them to the colored plastic dividers that came with binder. Use decorative paper clips to fasten your scrapbook page to the colored plastic page so that it becomes a unit.

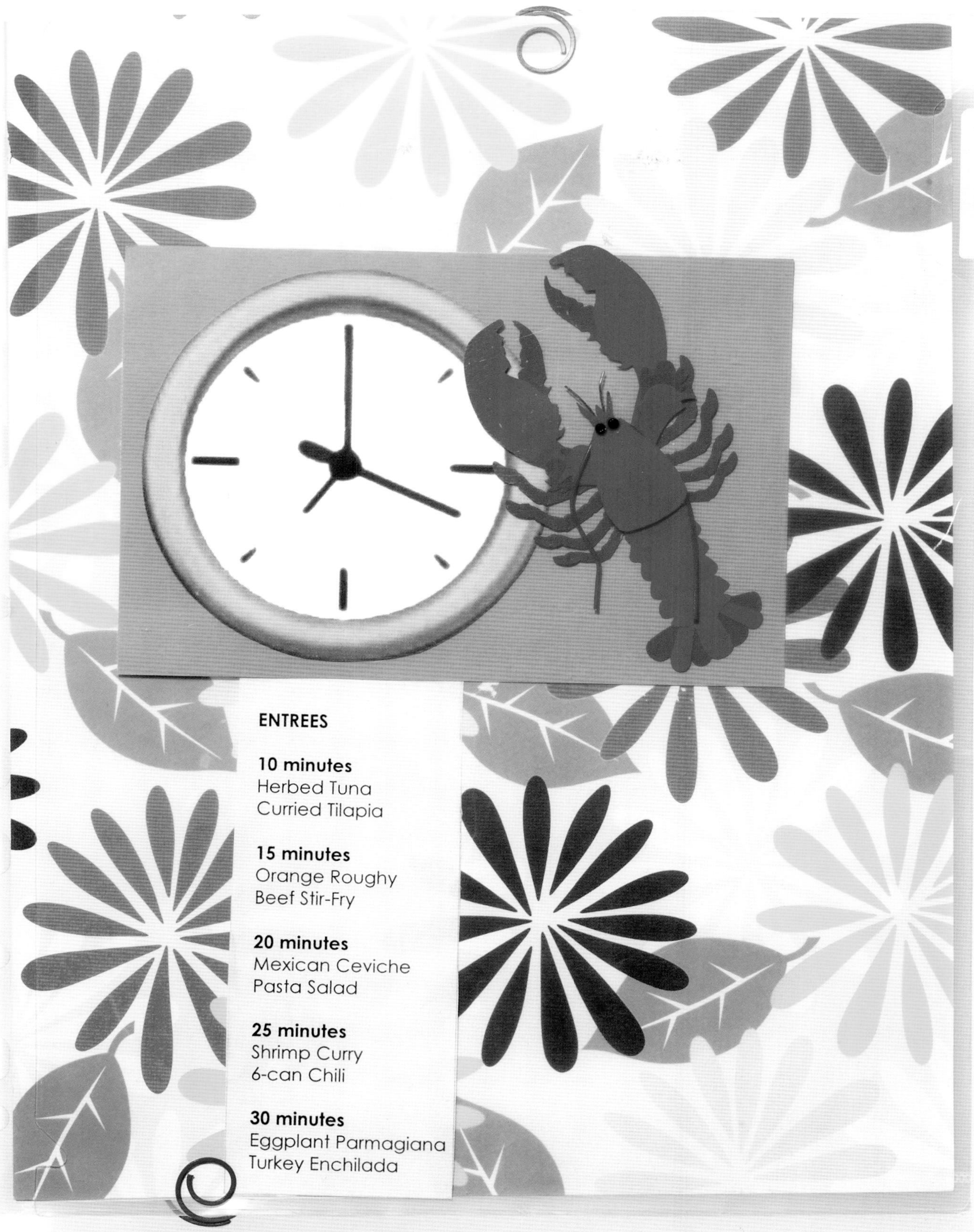
ENTREES
ENTREES
10 minutes
Herbed Tuna
Curried Tilapia
15 minutes
Orange Roughy
Beef Stir-Fry
20 minutes
Mexican Ceviche
Pasta Salad
25 minutes
Shrimp Curry
6-can Chili
30 minutes
Eggplant Parmagiana
Turkey Enchilada

Amusing stickers teamed with replicas of the cover clock are a lighthearted touch.

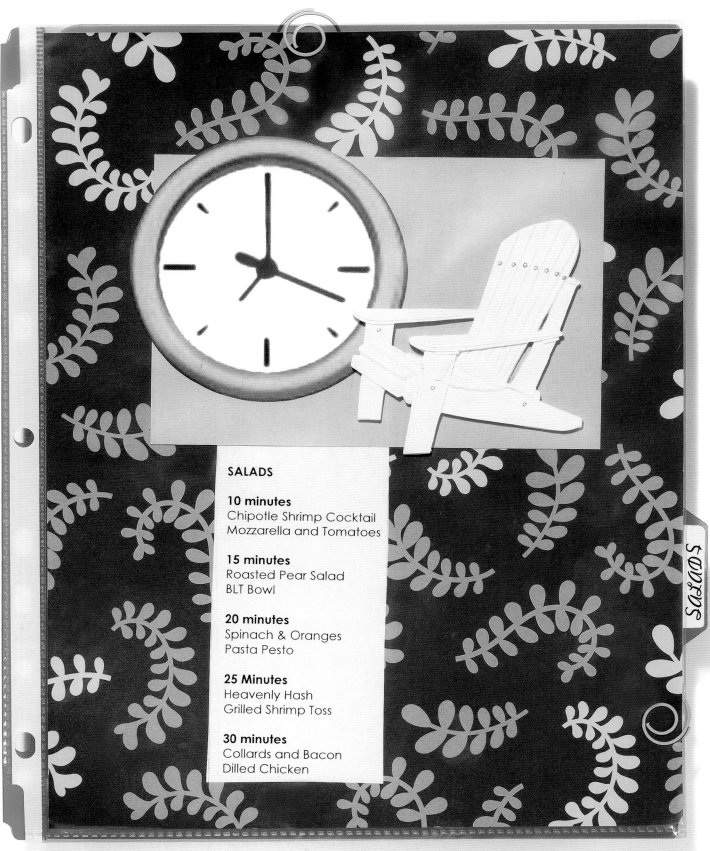

SALADS

10 minutes
Chipotle Shrimp Cocktail
Mozzarella and Tomatoes

15 minutes
Roasted Pear Salad
BLT Bowl

20 minutes
Spinach & Oranges
Pasta Pesto

25 Minutes
Heavenly Hash
Grilled Shrimp Toss

30 minutes
Collards and Bacon
Dilled Chicken

SALADS

SWEETS

10 minutes
Candy Cane Fudge
Coconut Truffles

15 minutes
White Chocolate Parfait
Caramel Pudding

20 minutes
Lemon Mousse

25 minutes
Cherries on a Cloud
Death by Chocolate

30 minutes
Oklahoma Mud
Raspberry Trifle

We found a series of retro patterns in stripes, florals, dots and checks. Just gluing the recipes onto these backgrounds gave the binder a hip new look in less than ten minutes.

According to crafter Pattie Donham, "Papers are to a scrapbooker what spices are to a cook. They can change the look of an album instantly and are a constant source of inspiration for me. For this book, I wanted something very playful, and somewhat unexpected. These papers had the offbeat colors and whimsical patterns I imagined, and coordinated very nicely with each other."

Pattie actually took her inspiration from her own kitchen, which is filled with retro touches like a Formica table, '50s-style fabrics and funky appliances. You could do something similar, putting together papers that echo your décor. Or take your cue from your spice cabinet and choose bold, earthy tones of paprika, cumin, basil and turmeric. Or be more subtle with a monochromatic palette—several different shades of green, for instance. A trip to the craft store or an Internet search will yield all sorts of possibilities.

Pattie also offers this suggestion: "Check out wrapping paper, wallpaper and fabric, too. You might be surprised at what you discover. Often I'll buy a wallpaper remnant and cut it to scrapbook size or use it for borders or mats. A small piece is enough to give a project a whole new spin. Sometimes it's even the jump-start for the project itself." ■ ■ ■

GET THE LOOK
The Pages

TO DO
● Coordinate background papers with appropriate dividers and simply glue recipes to them. Slip into plastic sleeves.

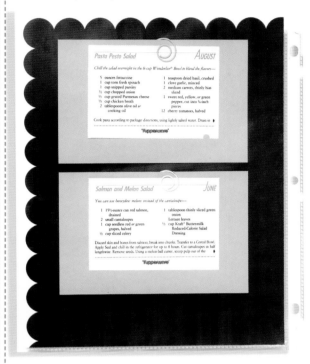

The hardest thing about making these is gluing the recipes onto the scrapbook pages. How easy is that?

SPECIAL GEAR
● **Scrapbook papers:** Stacy Claire Boyd for EK Success

Fillets of Fish Amandine

6 fish fillets — salt & pepper
Flour — 1½ cups butter
1 cup almonds, sliced — 1 lemon

Wipe fillets with damp cloth.
Sprinkle @ salt & pepper & dredge in
flour. Saute in ½ cup melted
butter until done but not too brown.
Place fillets in a pan. Mix almonds
& 1 cup melted butter. Heat until
almonds are light brown.
Pour almond mixture over fillets
& sprinkle @ lemon juice.
Place in 375° for 3 to 5 min
or until nicely browned.
Serve immediately.

Serves 6

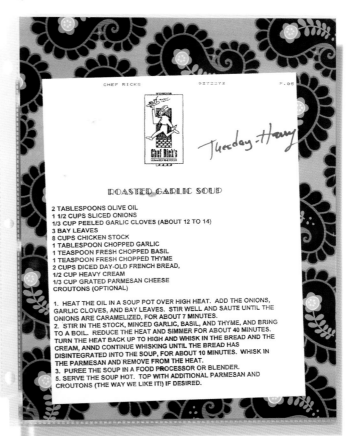

Chef Rick's
CULINARY FINE FOODS

Tuesday - Harry

ROASTED GARLIC SOUP

2 TABLESPOONS OLIVE OIL
1 1/2 CUPS SLICED ONIONS
1/3 CUP PEELED GARLIC CLOVES (ABOUT 12 TO 14)
3 BAY LEAVES
8 CUPS CHICKEN STOCK
1 TABLESPOON CHOPPED GARLIC
1 TEASPOON FRESH CHOPPED BASIL
1 TEASPOON FRESH CHOPPED THYME
2 CUPS DICED DAY-OLD FRENCH BREAD,
1/2 CUP HEAVY CREAM
1/3 CUP GRATED PARMESAN CHEESE
CROUTONS (OPTIONAL)

1. HEAT THE OIL IN A SOUP POT OVER HIGH HEAT. ADD THE ONIONS, GARLIC CLOVES, AND BAY LEAVES. STIR WELL AND SAUTE UNTIL THE ONIONS ARE CARAMELIZED, FOR ABOUT 7 MINUTES.
2. STIR IN THE STOCK, MINCED GARLIC, BASIL, AND THYME, AND BRING TO A BOIL. REDUCE THE HEAT AND SIMMER FOR ABOUT 40 MINUTES. TURN THE HEAT BACK UP TO HIGH AND WHISK IN THE BREAD AND THE CREAM, ANND CONTINUE WHISKING UNTIL THE BREAD HAS DISINTEGRATED INTO THE SOUP, FOR ABOUT 10 MINUTES. WHISK IN THE PARMESAN AND REMOVE FROM THE HEAT.
3. PUREE THE SOUP IN A FOOD PROCESSOR OR BLENDER.
5. SERVE THE SOUP HOT. TOP WITH ADDITIONAL PARMESAN AND CROUTONS (THE WAY WE LIKE IT!) IF DESIRED.

Pieces of coordinating construction paper add pizzazz.

CHECKS — LIST SINGLY — DOLLARS — CENTS

Sopapillas
1 pkg. yeast
1¼ C. warm water
1 tbsp. melted shortening
1 tbsp. sugar
4 C. flour
1 tsp. salt
Let rise until double
roll out the dough
Squares — fry
Dust up of powdered
sugar & Serve — Honey

TOTAL
ENTER TOTAL ON THE FRONT OF THIS TI...

Peach Cobbler

Crust: 2 C. flour
1 tsp. salt
⅔ C. Crisco
7 tbsp. cold water

Filling: ½ tsp. cinnamon
dash salt
Lemon juice
1 C. sugar
3 tbsp. flour

Sprinkle lemon juice over peaches.
Mix ingredients together and mix
with peaches. Pour in casserole
dish over crust. Dot with
butter and top with crust.
Slit & sprinkle with sugar
Bake flour at 350°

Blue Berry Pizza

Crust: 1 cup flour   350° oven
         1 stick butter (room temperature)
         2 tbsp sugar
Mix with hands & spread in pan
Bake about 10 minutes (watch closely)
Cream together: 8 oz. cream cheese
& spread on top   1 cup powdered sugar
of cooled crust   small carton Cool Whip
Top with Blueberry or Cherry pie filling

TECHNIQUE 101
Pompom Power

Pompoms are very easy to make. Although you can purchase a special pompom tool at a craft store, cardboard circles and a little sleight of hand will produce the same results.

Gather a variety of coordinating yarns.

Cut two cardboard circles to desired pompom size.

Cut holes in the center of both circles so they look like flat doughnuts. (Tip: The hole should be approximately one-third the size of the diameter of the pompom. So for a 1" pompom, the hole should be ⅓" wide.)

Place the cardboard circles on top of each other, making certain the holes line up.

Place end of one strand of yarn in hole and wrap around to edge and back again, winding around several times.

Take a coordinating strand and repeat process.

Continue repeating with different yarns until the center hole is full. Make sure yarn is distributed evenly around the circle with no lumps or bumps.

Place blade of scissors under the yarn at the edge of the circles and cut around cardboard until all yarn has been cut.

Pull the cardboard circles slightly apart and wrap a strand of yarn tightly between them, winding around a few times. Secure with a double knot and leave a length long enough to tie onto bookmark.

Make a slit in the cardboard circles and slip them out of the yarn. Fluff up the pompom. Trim any excess yarn.

Repeat process to make second pompom.

Attach pompoms to bookmark.

GET THE LOOK
Finishing Touches

TO DO

● Fasten alphabet stickers spelling out "simple suppers" (see page 35) on the solid side of a strip of scrapbook paper; punch a hole on one end. Laminate the paper at a copy center.

● Make a pompom with a pompom tool or by following instructions in "Technique 101" at left. Leave one piece of yarn long enough to slip through the punched hole.

TIP Instead of laminating, cut a strip of cardboard as a base for the bookmark. Glue scrapbook papers onto both sides of cardboard. With a single hole punch, make a hole at the top. Proceed to make a pompom as above.

A pompom bookmark makes it easy to keep your place.

DIFFERENT TAKES

Although we love the pompom idea, you could thread a bunch of buttons onto a chain or ribbon and use that to anchor the bookmark.

For an even simpler cover, just use one patterned scrapbook paper for the background and one solid paper for the title panel. Omit the words and the clock face, and simply stamp on your name or glue on self-stick letters.

Recipes to Try

Delicious dinners you can get on the table fast

Fish Baked in Foil

Serves 4

● This dish is very easy, very healthy, very tasty—and thanks to the foil packets, it requires minimal cleanup. What more could you want?

2 teaspoons grated orange peel

2 to 3 vine-ripened tomatoes, coarsely chopped

2 shallots, coarsely chopped

1 clove garlic, minced

2 tablespoons fresh basil, chopped

1 teaspoon crushed fennel seed

1/3 cup dry white wine

4 firm fish fillets (such as halibut, bass, cod, tilapia), 4–6 oz. each

4 sprigs fresh dill

Preheat oven to 350 degrees F.

In a small bowl, combine tomatoes, shallots, garlic, basil, fennel seed and wine.

Place each fish fillet on a piece of aluminum foil, fold up the sides slightly and top with some of the tomato mixture. Top each fillet with a sprig of dill. Fold foil securely over fillets.

Place in oven and cook 8–10 minutes or until fish flakes with a fork, but is still moist.

Lemon Herb Lamb

Serves 2

● Lamb chops cook in a flash, and if you pop them into this marinade night before or in the morning, you can have dinner on the table in no time.

1/4 cup olive oil (not extra-virgin), plus extra for pan broiling

1 tablespoon lemon juice

1 garlic clove, minced

1 teaspoon grated lemon zest

1 teaspoon fresh parsley, chopped

1 teaspoon fresh rosemary, chopped

1/4 teaspoon dried thyme

Salt and freshly ground black pepper, to taste

4 lamb rib chops, 1 inch thick

Mix together all ingredients, except for the lamb, and place in a resealable plastic bag. Add the chops, squishing around the marinade so all the meat is coated. Seal and refrigerate for at least two hours, or overnight.

Remove chops from bag and pat dry. Lightly coat a small skillet with oil and turn heat to medium-high. Once pan is hot, add chops and cook for 2–3 minutes or until browned. Turn chops over and brown on other side. Serve rare, or lower heat to medium and cook until chops reach desired doneness.

Holiday Hoopla

THE SPECIAL OCCASIONS ALBUM

Quick. Think of a holiday. Now think about what you do on that day. Chances are your answer involves food.

Whether it's burgers and hot dogs for a Memorial Day barbecue, charoset and matzoh ball soup for Passover, or a Christmas feast complete with different desserts, one of the major attractions of any holiday is the food. It's the link that binds the guests together, a ritual in and of itself. Which is why holiday menus can be harrowing for the cook—unlike other occasions, so much seems to rest on the food.

This cute felt house on the album's cover invites all to open the book and start browsing.

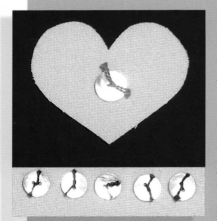

I can remember a disastrous Thanksgiving when the turkey took forever to cook and even my vast array of appetizers couldn't mellow the mood. At another time, I would have laughed, poured more wine and ordered out for pizza. But Thanksgiving means turkey, so I waited, along with my guests, each of us becoming crankier by the minute. Later on, after the dishes were washed and the leftovers stashed, I pondered the situation. Why such a big deal over some bird?

The answer lies in our love of tradition. A holiday—even a frivolous one like Valentine's Day——honors history and celebrates life. Unlike a simple dinner party, it's layered with meaning and touches our hearts in a most unique way. Because of this, I started a holiday "style file": a box where I stash photos of table settings, articles on entertaining, favorite menus and recipes. It's not ideal, but it is a help. No more rummaging around to find the stuffing everyone raved about or the website for authentic English plum pudding. But a book would be much handier, especially one with pockets for new recipes. So, based on that concept, we've *Cookbooked* a unique felt-covered album with convenient dividers for different holidays. You can include as many or as few holidays as you like, or nix the dividers and devote the book to one occasion. To give you an idea of how this may play out, we've zeroed in on the Thanksgiving festivities of my friend Cathleen Johnson, a public-relations executive in Chicago. Rather than do the day ➤

GET THE LOOK
The Cover

TO DO

● Start with a store-bought 12" by 12" scrapbook binder with screw-in posts.

● Iron an 18" x 52" piece of fusible interfacing onto a piece of heavy wool felt the exact same size, following interfacing manufacturer's instructions. Set aside.

● Select colors of assorted felt remnants for appliqués.

● Prepare appliqués with the felt and fusible webbing according to the method described in Technique 101.

● Once appliqués are in place, add decorative stitching around the edges using coordinating colors of embroidery floss. For more impact, use a few different stitches.
TIP You can find stitching guides on the Internet for inspiration. A few we like are at craftown.com, embroiderersguild.com and prettyimpressivestuff.com.

● Attach to cover using process described in Technique 101.

● Next, wrap the appliquéd cover around the album, securing with pins. Baste top and bottom edges together. Finish off with a simple running stitch in a contrasting color and remove basting threads.

● Embellish cover by tying embroidery floss through the buttonhole of a mother-of-pearl button, then affixing it onto window with glue dot.

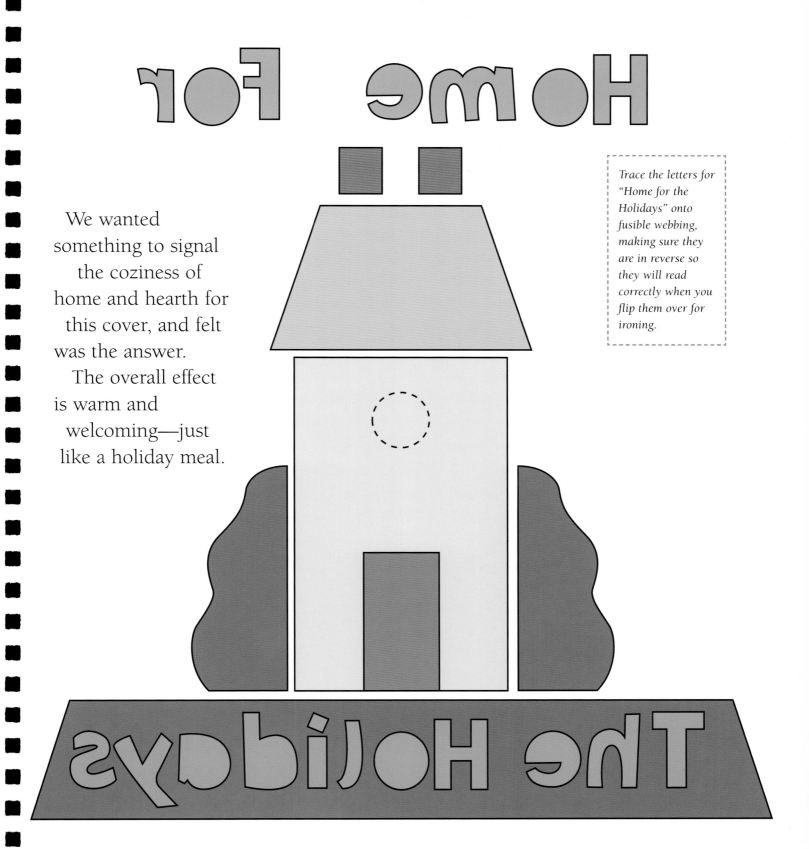

We wanted something to signal the coziness of home and hearth for this cover, and felt was the answer.

The overall effect is warm and welcoming—just like a holiday meal.

Trace the letters for "Home for the Holidays" onto fusible webbing, making sure they are in reverse so they will read correctly when you flip them over for ironing.

the traditional way, Cathleen celebrates with a glorious progressive dinner that's a grand idea in itself. Now she has an album to encourage the making of other fabulous holiday meals.

THE INSPIRATION

The next time Thanksgiving rolls around, I want to be invited to celebrate with my friend Cathleen. She and her brother and sister have tweaked tradition by turning Turkey Day into a marvelous movable feast.

"The three of us have weekend places on Lake Geneva, Wisconsin, and we're always visiting each other, so a progressive dinner seemed like a good idea—a great way to split up the work and have fun at the same time," says Cathleen. "The downside is I always have an extra dessert because I rationalize that the walking burns up calories."

Cathleen and her siblings have kept up the ritual for six years now, with friends and extended family joining the festivities. The plan works like this: appetizers and drinks at one stop, dinner at the "host house," then dessert at the third. "Every year we switch around the assignments and try to shake things up with new recipes and new presentations. Once we painted the tackiest turkey silhouettes onto cheap white aprons, using our hands for the outline, and wore them throughout the day. Another time, we cut out pictures of celebrities for place cards and guests were supposed to sit down at their ➤

The Dividers

TO DO

- Cut pieces of felt, 13" x 13", for each divider.

- Cut coordinating pieces of felt, 13" x 6½", for each pocket.

- Cut felt appliqués, following instructions in Technique 101.

- Embellish appliqués and pockets as desired with mother-of-pearl buttons.

- Baste the "pockets" onto the dividers, continuing around the side and top of the larger piece of felt.

- Finish off with a simple running stitch in a contrasting embroidery floss. Remove basting threads. Accent pockets with more buttons by either stitching onto the felt or by tying floss through the buttonholes and affixing with glue dots.

- Trim the edges of the dividers with pinking shears before inserting into book.

> **SPECIAL GEAR**
> **Felt:** Ours is a selection of vintage remnants found at quilt and flea markets. New felt works as well but is not as soft, so you may want to wash it first.

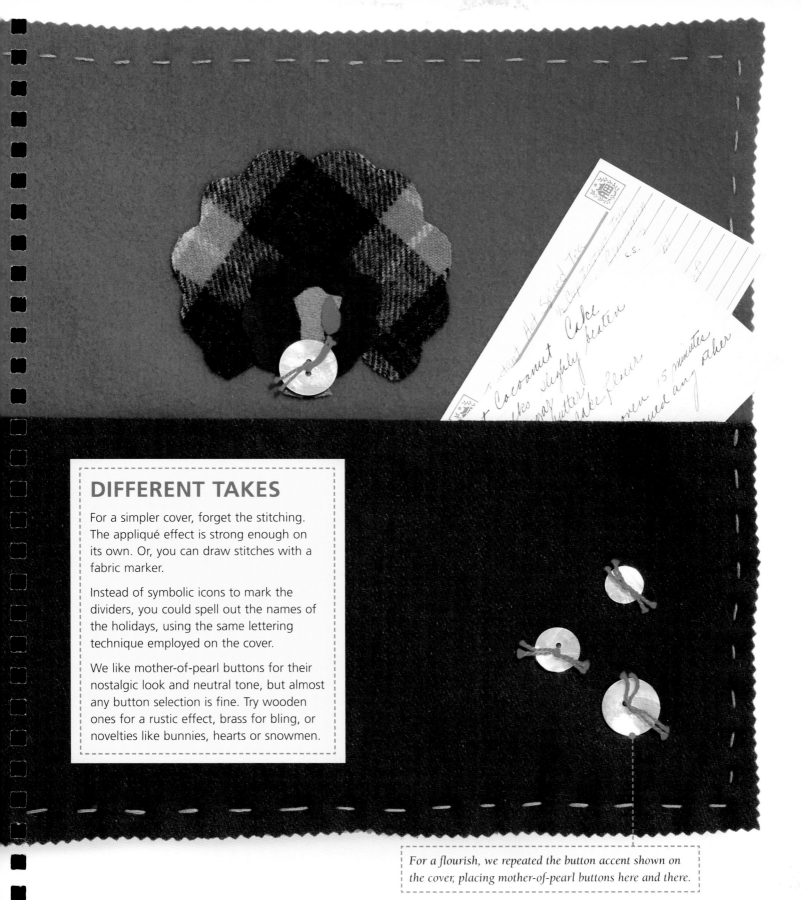

DIFFERENT TAKES

For a simpler cover, forget the stitching. The appliqué effect is strong enough on its own. Or, you can draw stitches with a fabric marker.

Instead of symbolic icons to mark the dividers, you could spell out the names of the holidays, using the same lettering technique employed on the cover.

We like mother-of-pearl buttons for their nostalgic look and neutral tone, but almost any button selection is fine. Try wooden ones for a rustic effect, brass for bling, or novelties like bunnies, hearts or snowmen.

For a flourish, we repeated the button accent shown on the cover, placing mother-of-pearl buttons here and there.

From the house on the cover to the funny turkey and snowman on the divider pages, appliqués give this book a homespun look that's very appealing.

Sketch shapes of your various appliqués onto the paper side of ¼ yard of fusible webbing. (You can either draw freehand or download templates.)

Cut around the shapes, leaving at least 1 " all around.

Iron the fusible shapes onto your selected pieces of felt, then trim along the outlines.

Arrange appliqués for proper position and lightly outline with a pencil.

Peel the paper off the appliqués and iron onto the felt, following your penciled outline. To prevent scorching, use a handkerchief or pressing cloth.

You can see why Cathleen loves the dividers: marked with whimsical appliqués representing the different holidays, they sport nifty pockets to hold new recipes.

look-alike's setting. It was a riot when all the guys chose Steve McQueen," laughs Cathleen.

In 2004 Cathleen was in charge of the main event, and she was very apprehensive. "I'm great at mixing drinks and choosing cheeses, but being responsible for the feast had me panicked," she says. "My sister Barb and I are reputed to be terrible cooks, so my nephew Zach kept e-mailing me recipes he found on the Internet. I think it was his way of assuring that there would be something edible on the table."

Zach, who is blessed with a great sense of humor, also made a sign to hang at the front of the house stating "Dinner is here, have no fear."

But, to everyone's surprise, the meal was excellent, and Cathleen is on the agenda to do it again. "Thankfully people have forgotten the time I omitted the sugar in the pumpkin/chocolate pie, or the day I roasted the turkey with the giblets still inside," she says. "Then again, there are those who have excellent memories. My family refers to them as 'one-time guests.'"

Now, thanks to *Cookbooking*, Cath has an album for recording future festivities. "The thing I love best is the pockets on each divider," she says. "I can download something from my computer or clip a page from a magazine and simply tuck it into the pocket. Sign me up for Christmas!" ■ ■ ■

GET THE LOOK
The Pages

TO DO

● Select 12" x 12" textured scrapbook papers to set off recipes, menus and photos.

● **For text pages**: Print out menus, comments, guest lists, etc., on 8½" x 11" coordinating papers using fonts of your choice. Center and glue onto scrapbook papers. With glue dots, affix buttons tied with colorful embroidery floss at edges, corners, or wherever desired.

● **For recipe pages**: With glue dots, affix floss-tied buttons to the top center of the scrapbook papers. Place computer printouts or handwritten recipes under the buttons.
TIP Do not glue the recipes; you may want to slip them out to use when cooking.

● **For photo pages**: Glue photos into desired arrangement on a contrasting colored paper you've trimmed with decorative shears. Adorn by adding decorative stitches and buttons. Write special comments with a fine-line gold paint pen. Glue onto scrapbook papers.

● Slip completed pages into 12" x 12" top-loading page protectors.

● Organize pages into correct order and place in album with the screw-in posts.

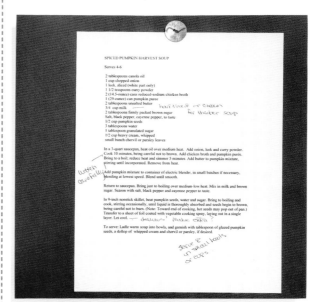

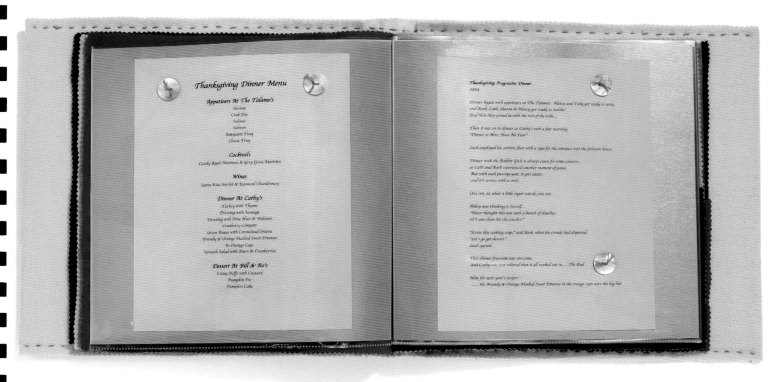

The papers for this album are beautifully textured for a subtle yet sumptuous background. Embellishments are minimal: just more buttons— singles to anchor the recipes and clusters to accent the photo pages.

Recipes to Try

Classics updated—that's the key to a scrumptious holiday meal

Roast Turkey with Herbs and Herb Butter

Serves 8

● Everyone has a favorite way of roasting a turkey, and this is mine. The butter-soaked cheesecloth helps keeps the turkey skin from burning, and herb butter infuses the bird with flavor.

12-lb. fresh turkey, preferably organic

Kosher salt

1 lemon, cut in quarters

5 sprigs fresh rosemary

5 sprigs fresh thyme

10 fresh sage leaves

½ cup softened butter, plus ½ cup melted butter

1 tablespoon fresh rosemary, chopped

1 tablespoon fresh sage, chopped

1 tablespoon fresh thyme, chopped

1 teaspoon lemon zest, finely grated

½ teaspoon fresh ground black pepper

Preheat oven to 350 degrees F.

Remove gizzards from cavity of turkey and discard.

Rinse bird well and pat dry. Season cavity with kosher salt; place lemon wedges and rosemary sprigs inside cavity.

In a small bowl, blend the ½ cup softened butter, herbs, lemon zest and pepper until well mixed.

Working carefully so you do not tear the turkey skin, slide your hand under the skin of the turkey breast to loosen it. Then, with fingers, smear butter under the skin, doing one side of the breast at a time. Work slowly, smearing the butter as far as it will go under the skin. Smear remaining herbed butter over neck, leg and back of the turkey.

Tie legs of the bird together with kitchen twine; tuck wing tips under the body and place the turkey on a rack inside roasting pan and cook for about 30 minutes. At this point, dip a piece of cheesecloth (large enough to lay over top of turkey) in melted butter; place over turkey. In another 20–30 minutes, remove the cheesecloth and coat with more melted butter. Repeat again at 20–30-minute intervals. Turkey is cooked when meat thermometer registers 180 degrees when inserted into thickest part of thigh, about 3 hours.

Remove turkey from oven, cover with foil and let rest at least 15 minutes before serving.

Spinach Salad with Pears and Cranberries

Serves 1-2

● Cathleen likes serving a salad at the Thanksgiving table because it offers a refreshing balance to the heavier dishes and makes her "feel healthier." If you want more crunch, add ½ cup chopped walnuts.

2 teaspoons grated orange peel

1 cup orange juice

1 cup seasoned rice vinegar

1 cup dried cranberries

4 firm, ripe pears, cored and thinly sliced

1 ½ cups red onion, thinly sliced

2 lbs. baby spinach leaves, washed

In a large bowl, mix orange peel, orange juice, vinegar and dried cranberries. Add sliced pears and onions and stir until well coated.

Cover and chill for at least one hour. Just before serving, place spinach in salad bowl, add pear mixture and toss gently.

Roasted Sweet Potatoes

Serves 8

● These sweet potatoes are a classy alternative to the candy-like brown sugar/marshmallow/sweet potato casserole that so many of us grew up with. The roasting lends a nice smoky flavor, while the cinnamon and honey impart just enough sweetness.

4 tablespoons butter, melted + extra for drizzling

4 tablespoons honey

2 tablespoon fresh lime juice

4 teaspoon ground cinnamon

8 medium sweet potatoes, peeled and sliced into 1 inch strips

Nonstick cooking spray

Salt and pepper to taste

Preheat oven to 400 degrees F.

Blend butter, honey, lime juice and cinnamon in a large bowl. Add potato slices; toss to coat. Arrange potato slices in single layer on baking sheet sprayed with cooking spray. Sprinkle with salt and pepper. Roast until tender, about 25 minutes.

Remove from oven, place on platter and drizzle with more melted butter before serving.

Cornbread, Mushroom and Pancetta Stuffing

Serves 12

● Technically this is not a stuffing because you cook it in a separate dish, but whatever the name, it tastes delicious.

1 package (16 oz.) cornbread stuffing mix

12 oz. pancetta, diced

3 cups white onion, diced

2 cups celery, diced

1 lb. portobello or cremini mushrooms, diced

1 teaspoon dried sage

½ teaspoon oregano

½ teaspoon salt

1 teaspoon black pepper, freshly ground

½ cup fresh parsley, chopped

4 eggs

½ cup dry white wine

2 cups chicken broth

1 tablespoon butter

Heat oven to 350 degrees F. Lightly butter a 13" x 9" x 2" baking dish.

Cook pancetta in a deep skillet until golden brown. Drain off most of the fat, leaving about 1 tablespoon in pan.

Add onion and celery; sauté until softened and lightly browned, about 5 minutes. Add mushrooms, stirring gently, and cook 5 minutes. Add herbs, salt and pepper; stir and cook for 1 minute.

Put stuffing mix and parsley into a large bowl; add mixture from pan.

In a small bowl, whisk eggs and wine. Transfer to bowl with stuffing.

Next, add half the broth and mix gently. Pour in rest of broth, a little at a time, stirring as you go.

Put in prepared baking dish. Dot with butter. Cover with aluminum foil.

Bake 45 minutes or until lightly browned. Uncover; let stand 10 minutes. Serve immediately.

As pretty as a candy box from a high-end confectionery, this elegant book is a treat in itself.

Crazy for Chocolate
THE CHOCOLATE BOOK

Decadent. Sinful. Indulgent. To die for. In the world of food, only chocolate provokes such descriptions. And only chocolate can claim so many fans. For some, just the thought may induce a swoon. For others, a day without is not to be contemplated. Like its floral counterpart the rose, chocolate has inspired poems, songs, movies and books, and its enthusiasts are quite articulate about the object of their affection. Years ago, a shy, rather awkward assistant in my office stunned me with her account of the perfect truffle. This extremely quiet young woman launched into a brilliant soliloquy about "achingly" bittersweet cocoa, "velvety" ganache and "not-to-be-denied excess." All of a sudden she was confident, poised and extremely eloquent. Whatever she ordered, I wanted the same.

Yet although I like chocolate—a lot!—I would never label myself a chocoholic. Truth be told, if I had a choice between a lemon tart and chocolate cake, I'd pick the tart at least 70 percent of the time. But I've learned that I'm in the minority. And I do agree that the best dessert to serve at a dinner party is a chocolate one. It can redeem even the blandest of meals. Everyone will leave on a chocolate high, forgetting that the lamb was ➤

too well-done and the potatoes au gratin too soggy. For me, the dessert to bring out is Nigella Lawson's Molten Chocolate Baby Cakes. They're easy, they're make-ahead, they're beyond scrumptious. And people always request the recipe. In fact, they were the inspiration for this next *Cookbooking* concept—a collection of chocolate recipes, chocolate lore, chocolate facts. Designed to give as a gift, this tasty compendium is deluxe all the way, with lush papers and lavish accents. What a nice present for the chocolate lovers in my life!

THE INSPIRATION

Once we hit upon the idea of a gift book, the rest fell into place. The book needed to look rich and abundant, exuding the same sense of luxury as high-end chocolates. Immediately the idea of chocolate labels came to mind. Think Godiva, Ghirardelli, Guylian, Teuscher. Neuhaus. These would be ideal embellishments. And the best part was we'd need to eat the chocolates in order to collect the labels! Even the recipes called ➤

The Cover

TO DO

- Start by assembling a mix of photos from magazines, from the Internet, even from the lids of chocolate boxes. Scan onto your computer and take to a photo processing center for reproduction. This will assure an even consistency. (Request a glossy finish for the sleekest result.)

- Cut two pieces of 8" x 8" foamcore for front and back covers.

- Cut three pieces of 8" x 8" textured brown paper. With spray adhesive, adhere one to back of front cover, others to front and back of second piece of foamcore to form back cover.

- Apply foiling glue to edges of covers, let dry, then apply gold foiling, pressing down consistently for a smooth golden edge that resembles the foil around a chocolate bar.
  TIP Since foiling glue needs a couple of hours to dry, you can speed things up by using 1/8" double-sided foiling tape instead.

- Place front cover over back and make a pencil mark at upper left-hand corner where you want grommets to be. Using a brass grommet kit and manufacturer's directions, set grommets into both front and back covers.

- Cut a piece of 8" x 8" acetate, and with a single-hole punch make a hole in upper left-hand corner to match up with grommet. (This will help protect and give an added sheen to your cover.)

SPECIAL GEAR
- **Gold foiling:** PattiWack Designs
- **Brads:** Spare Parts by The Paper Studio
- **Rub-ons:** ChartPak

If this doesn't trigger a chocolate craving, what will?
The collage of bonbons, cupcakes, chocolate bars and
icing clearly indicates what this book is all about.

We've fashioned a
stylish vellum tag
labeled "Chocolate"
in shimmery,
glimmery gold.

Make a collage of your
photos using the method
described in Technique 101.

classy treatment. No computer printouts or magazine clippings here. This was the place for calligraphy, written on sheets of elegant vellum.

Some lore and legend also seemed appropriate because true chocolate lovers justify their cravings with all sorts of arcane knowledge. I googled "chocolate lore" and "chocolate facts" and discovered dozens of sites with fascinating information, any of which would add interest to the book. For instance, did you know that the ancient Mayans considered cacao beans so precious they used them as currency? Or that chocolate was such a luxury during the reign of Louis XIV that he established a position known as Royal Chocolate Maker to the King? Or, that chocolate is known as the "love drug" because it contains phenylethylamine, a mood-elevating substance that mimics the brain chemistry of a person in love?

There's also the tale about the guy who found a bottle in the ocean and out popped a genie who granted him three wishes. The guy requested a million dollars, and poof! the cash appeared. He wished for a Jaguar convertible, and poof! there it was. Then, he asked to be irresistible to women, and poof! he turned into a box of chocolates. ➤

GET THE LOOK
The Pages

TO DO

- Select an assortment of different scrapbook papers in tones of chocolate, coffee, copper. Go for texture, with mottled, ribbed and striated finishes.

- Cut papers to 8" x 8".

- **Photo pages**: Select photos from magazines, boxes, and the Internet and take to a photo processing center for reproduction. As with the cover, ask for a glossy finish.

- Cut photos to desired size and attach to papers with small scrapbooking brads.

- Affix labels from chocolate candy on selected pages with a glue stick.

- Afflix metallic sticker letters where desired, spelling out words and phrases such as "pick one" or "sweet."

- Write short quotes with a fine-line gold paint pen on pieces of gold vellum.

- Use black rub-on embellishments (fleurs-de-lis, scrolls, etc.) to fancy up corners and borders of the vellum. Attach next to photos with decorative scrapbooking brads.

- Back all pages that contain brads with patterned

- Line up pages with cover and mark correct hole placement. Form holes with single-hole punch.

May your road be paved with *Chocolate*

May your road be paved with chocolate – bittersweet
to journey through exotic lands of mystery and
intrigue, silks and satins, perfumes and spices,
and women with almond eyes; milk chocolate
for warm, lazy days, drifting down river,
the sun on your back, fingers trailing in cool water,
an icy drink by your side and a straw hat pushed
low on your forehead; semi-sweet for fields of
lavender, the snowy crest of the Matterhorn,
moonlight on the beach, and Paris in the
spring; white chocolate to relax on a velvet
sofa, wear shimmering organza, sip
Dom Perignon, eat caviar on ridiculously
tiny toast points and dance to Frank and Ella
until the wee hours of the morning.

Whatever you do and wherever you go,
whether near or far or in between, may your
road be paved with chocolate for flattery will
get you nowhere; chocolate, everywhere.

Nanette Littlestone

Intro page: *Print out an essay or poem of your choice onto embossed vellum.*

Recipe pages: *Handwrite recipes with a fine-line gold paint pen on gold or white vellum. Accent with rub-on enhancements if desired.* **TIP** *To make reading easier, follow any vellum recipe page with a page of ivory cardstock. Do not glue; simply insert into appropriate place.*

Fact page: *Clip out text on chocolate facts from magazines and with a glue stick adhere in a random pattern on a single page. Cut out descriptive words and phrases such as "decadence" and "a chocolate dream" and affix with square resin stickers. Fancy up with a photo adhered with a glue stick.* **TIP** *You could also print out chocolate information from your computer in the font of your choice and cut into desired sizes.*

Marble Brownie
1 pkg. Brownie Mix
1 pkg. Cream Cheese
1/3 cup sugar
1 egg
1 tsp. vanilla

Prepare brownie mix as directed on package. Pour into greased 13 x 9 inch baking pan.

Beat cream cheese on medium speed until smooth. Add sugar, mixing until blended. Add egg & vanilla, mix just until blended.

Pour cheese mixture over brownie mixture. Cut through batter with knife several times for marble effect.

Bake at 350° for 35 to 40 minutes until lightly browned. Cool, cut into squares.

Turn the pages, and you're treated to luscious bits of chocolate lore and photographs as well as mouth-watering quotes. Even if you're not ready to make fondue or brownies, leafing through this book is a treat.

A Day without Chocolate is like a Day without Sunshine

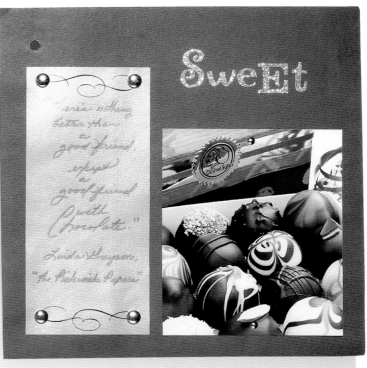

SweEt

"There is nothing better than a good friend, except a good friend with Chocolate."

Linda Grayson,
"The Pickwick Papers"

70% AFRICAN EBONY
GuyLiAN SOLITAIRE

70% AFRICAN EBONY
GuyLiAN SOLITAIRE

pIck ONe

Forget about Love... I'd rather fall in Chocolate

TECHNIQUE 101

Collage Cues

Fashioning a collage of photos like the one on this cover is simple if you use a trick or two. Here's the way to do it.

Cut a piece of posterboard 12" x 12", then cut out an 8" x 8" opening in the center to form a frame.

Move your photos around, overlapping here and there, then lay the frame over them to study placement. Experiment until you find an arrangement that's pleasing.

With a pencil, mark where photos will be cropped, then trim to preferred size.

Interestingly enough, when Christopher Columbus discovered cocoa beans in the New World, nobody cared. English and Dutch sailors who plundered Spanish galleons assumed the beans were sheep's droppings and threw them overboard. Then, in the mid-1800s a process was devised for turning them into solid chocolate, and chocolate bars and bonbons became the rage.

Imagine.—hundreds of years wasted because nobody knew what to do with the beans. But this book will help a friend do a little catching up. Filled with tips, facts, recipes and evocative photos, it will satiate the most avid chocoholic. Well, almost—we suggest presenting it along with a box of—what else?—chocolates. ■ ■ ■

GET THE LOOK
Finishing Touches

TO DO

● **Ring:** Cover a 2 ½" metal ring with gold braid.

● **Tag:** Cut a piece of heavy white vellum into a tag shape, approximately 8" long. Punch a hole at the top. Apply metallic sticker letters to spell out the word "chocolate."

● Trim with gold foiling, the same way you did for the edges of cover.

● **Tassel**: Use a tassel tool to fashion a tassel with yarn and fibers in shades of gold, silver, copper, brown. Top with a coordinating bead.

● Connect everything together with metal ring.

DIFFERENT TAKES

For an easier cover approach, zero in on just one shot—a closeup of a big, dark bar of chocolate, perhaps. A photo of an opened box of truffles would also work, as would a pile of brownies, a slice of chocolate cake, anything that's up close and personal.

Fancy up the ring with metallic or glass beads in tones of gold for a more flamboyant effect.

Rather than writing the recipes on vellum, do in white ink on deep brown paper. Another option is to mount the recipes on scrapbook papers. Just cut vellum to size, choose dark brown or gold ink, and attach to papers with brads. Placed next to a photo or series of labels, this is very effective and will cut down on the number of pages.

Recipes to Try

Take a bite. And another.
And another.
Bliss is yours.

Chocolate-Apricot Tart

Serves 6–8

● The double hit of chocolate—in the crust and in the filling—makes this a chocolate lover's delight. If apricots aren't your thing, substitute orange marmalade for the jam and top the tart with freshly cut orange slices.

3 dozen chocolate wafer cookies

6 tablespoons unsalted butter, slightly softened

8 oz. bittersweet chocolate, chopped

1 cup heavy cream

1 cup whole dried apricots

½ cup apricot brandy

⅓ cup seedless apricot jam

Place cookies in a large, resealable plastic bag and crush with a rolling pin until finely ground. Mix cookie crumbs and butter in a medium bowl. Press crumb mixture over bottom and up sides of a 9" tart pan with removable bottom.

Heat the jam in a small saucepan over low heat until just melted. Pour over the bottom of tart shell. Freeze for 15 minutes.

Meanwhile, warm the chocolate and cream in a double boiler over low heat until all the chocolate is melted and the mixture is smooth. Pour into frozen tart shell.

Refrigerate until chocolate is set, about 4 hours.

Slice apricots into halves and pour apricot brandy over them; let them soak for 30 minutes until soft. Set aside.

Once tart has set, arrange apricots on top. Refrigerate until ready to serve.

Grandma's Mistakes

Makes approximately 25 bars

● My friend Gina, who hails from Michigan, started making this recipe back home, and thankfully has brought it along with her to New York. She's as mystified by the name as I am, but who cares? These bar cookies are better than any other—bar none!

1 cup butter

1 cup flour

1 cup brown sugar

2 cups old-fashioned oats

½ teaspoon baking soda

½ cup butter

12 ounces chocolate chips

1 can sweetened condensed milk

Preheat oven to 350 degrees F. Mix together first 5 ingredients and press ¾ of mixture into 9" x 13" baking pan. In saucepan over low heat, melt butter, chocolate chips and milk. Pour chocolate mixture over oatmeal layer and crumble remaining oatmeal mixture on top. Bake for 25 minutes. Cool slightly; cut into rectangles.

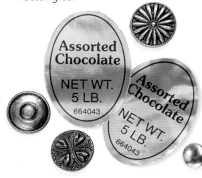

Shaken, Not Stirred

THE COCKTAIL FOLDOUT

After decades of taking a backseat to wine, the cocktail has made a definite comeback. People now order all kinds of mixed drinks, restaurants offer lists of flavored martinis and bartenders are no longer called bartenders—they are mixologists. Even the *New York Times* has a regular column devoted to the drink of the moment. I credit this trend to the four women of *Sex and the City* and their passion for Cosmopolitans, but who knows? Everyone seems to have a favorite cocktail and will pay a stiff price to get it.

The fad has also traveled home. These days, dinner parties often begin with a "Welcome Cocktail." It sets a festive feeling, puts people in a good mood and gets the conversation rolling. "Girls' Night In" is another popular concept. I first learned about this from Joan Fee, a pal in Fresno, California. "Rather than meeting my friends at a local club or lounge, we now get together at one of our homes. The hostess provides the drinks, the guests bring the snacks and we all just gab the night away," she explains. "It's more relaxing than a restaurant, ➤

The Cover

TO DO

- Purchase a plain accordion book, cut sheet of chosen scrapbook paper to size; affix with glue stick to the cover.

- Pencil outline of martini glass onto paper.

- Apply foiling glue around outline of glass; let set until glue becomes tacky.

- Press crafting foil into place on the glue outline. **TIP** For something quicker, nix the foil and use glitter.

- Embellish the rest of the cover with self-stick gems (two act as the "olives" in the glass) and rub-on words "best friends."

- Use label maker to spell out "cocktails"; affix in place with glue stick.

As easy as pouring vodka—just glue on some glittery gems to slick up the back pages of the book

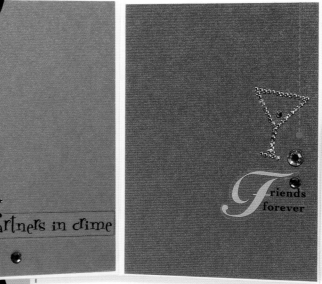

An outline of a martini glass immediately lets you know what this is all about.

best
friends
COCKTAILS

This glammed-up foldout includes tried and tested recipes for luscious cocktails plus photos of get-togethers with friends. Cheers!

and a whole lot gentler on the pocketbook."

Since Joan is a crafter—she does everything from découpage to quilting—she came up with the idea of collecting all of the cocktail recipes from an evening and putting them together in a book. Simply cut and paste, add some photos, and there you have it: a perfect reference for future parties as well as a memory book.

THE INSPIRATION

Joan's cocktail fold-out is a testament to her joy for life. A writer for a large crafts company, she's affectionately referred to as Party Girl. "I guess I'm a real social animal, because bringing people together is one of my greatest pleasures," she says. "Even if it's just a casual rendezvous at my place, I'll stop off at the dollar store to pick up some funny favors and concoct a special cocktail to break the ice."

Her Girls' Night In events are actually a shorter version of the Women-Only Weekends she used to enjoy. "For years, my mother, sister, sister-in-law and friends would set aside a couple of days to spend together—sans husbands, boyfriends, children. Sometimes we'd go to a spa, other times we'd just a rent a place, take walks and cook and craft together. There would always be a lot of giggling and just the right amount of soul-searching. Afterwards, we'd all go back to our real lives feeling recharged and renewed."

Girls' Night In fetes can do the same thing. Who can resist a cocktail or two, some tasty noshes and the company of close friends? Joan suggests coming ➤

The Pages

TO DO

- Select scrapbook papers in a coordinating color palette (ours is frosty blue and silver for recipe pages and violet and kiwi for the back).

- Cut papers to size and affix to accordion book with a glue stick, except for the last page.

- Before affixing paper to the last page, cut two strips of ribbon, each about 20" long, and glue onto book. These ribbons will act as the ties. Affix scrapbook paper over the ribbons.

- Select cardstock in colors that coordinate with your scrapbook papers as backgrounds for photos and recipes. (We used raspberry for the recipes and violet for the photos.)

- Print cocktail recipes on plain white copy paper, using colored ink that matches your cardstock.

- Cut out recipes and affix them to slightly larger pieces of the colored cardstock, then affix to book with glue stick.

- Adorn pages with self-stick gems, martini-glass stickers, rub-on words and so on.

- Add a favorite saying about friendship by printing one on cardstock, or find a pre-printed self-adhesive one, such as "A friend is someone who knows all about you and loves you just the same."

- As a final touch, glue "olives" cut from green and red paper here and there. (Use a single-hole punch for the pimientos.) As Joan says, "When my girlfriends and I get together, we must have olives. I even cured my own a couple of years ago, and I think in my next life I'll come back as the Olive Queen."

SPECIAL GEAR
Rhinestone stickers: Me&MyBig Ideas

it's our Secret

MICHELLE
STACEY

Chocolate Kiss

1 1/2 oz. crème de cacao
1/2 oz. cream
Fill a rocks glass with ice
Add ingredients
Stir well
Kiss quickly

Lauren's Fuzzy Navel

1 oz. Peach Schnapps
Orange Juice
Ice
9 oz. glass

Add ice
Add schnapps
Fill with orange juice
Look out!

Sassy

LAUREN

Favorite recipes and fun embellishments jazz up the pages.

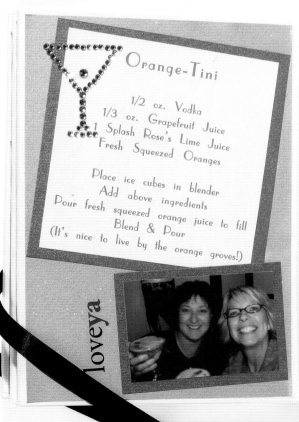

Orange-Tini

1/2 oz. Vodka
1/3 oz. Grapefruit Juice
1 Splash Rose's Lime Juice
Fresh Squeezed Oranges

Place ice cubes in blender
Add above ingredients
Pour fresh squeezed orange juice to fill
Blend & Pour
(It's nice to live by the orange groves!)

loveya

girlfriends

A friend is someone who knows all about you and LOVES YOU just the same.
- Elbert Hubbard

To reinforce your tailor-made paper foldout, cut two pieces of cardstock to size and affix to first and last pages with a glue stick.Use a bone folder to crease the edges of the glued cover.

GET THE LOOK
Make It Custom

Although plain accordion books are fairly easy to find, you can make your own—a good idea if you want a particular size, like a mini-book of recipes to present to guests.

Start by figuring out what dimensions you want for your pages, then multiply the width by eight to find the length of paper you will need for your book. For instance, if you want a book that's 4" wide and 5" high, you'll need a 32" sheet of paper. Select your paper: You can use very stiff paper or tagboard. Cut to height of your page (in this case 5"). See A.

 A

Fold paper in half, so that it is now 16" x 5", and crease with a bone folder. See B.

 B

Fold the left side of paper in half again to meet the center fold, creasing new fold with bone folder. See C.

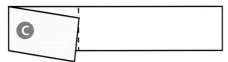

Now reverse direction of this fold. (This double folding will give the right flexibility.)

Fold the new fold to meet the center fold, so this left side is now folded in quarters. See D.

Repeat with other half of sheet of paper. This will result in 8 panels. See E.

up with a theme for the drinks: Island Paradise, perhaps, with tropical treats such as Daiquiris and Mai Tais, or 1940s Glamour with Manhattans, Martinis and Gimlets. Or, mix up a whole range of drinks based on only one kind of liquor. "The simplest thing to do is splurge on a lovely bottle of port. A couple of friends bring cheese, others bring fruit and crackers, and we just sip and savor the moment."

On the other hand, if you want to go all out, that's fine too. "Since I'm a crafter, I make my invitations and party items," says Joan. "Give me some paper and glue, and I'm on." In fact, after looking at this book, Joan decided it would be fun to do versions with blank pages that can be filled in with future get-togethers. ■ ■ ■

Even a paper-crafting novice can do this project: Just begin with a plain accordion book, set up a work surface for cutting and gluing and go from there. It's that easy.

GET THE LOOK
Finishing Touches

TO DO

● Grab a classic label maker to spell out names of friends and affix to their photos.

● Adorn back pages with more gems, martini stickers and other sayings relating to friendship.

DIFFERENT TAKES

For a more glamorous effect, choose scrapbook papers in black, silver and iridescent white. Adorn with faux rhinestones and black and white feathers.

We love the accordion format, but square pages held together by a single ring at the top corner also work well for a small book like this.

Add blank sheets of paper and pass around at a "Girls' Night In" so that friends can write down personal comments.

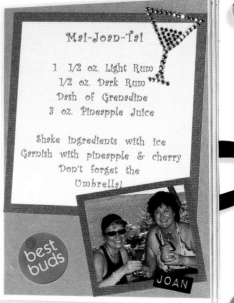

Recipes to Try

When a glass of wine just isn't special enough, try one of these.

The Ultimate Margarita

Serves 1

Everyone seems to make this south-of-the-border treat a different way, but this uses the classic 3-2-1 ratio and it's a doozy. Triple Sec can be substituted for Cointreau, but the result is slightly less smooth.

2 lime wedges

Coarse salt

1 ½ oz. white tequila (100 percent agave)

1 oz. Cointreau

½ oz. freshly squeezed lime juice

Sugar to taste

Ice cubes

Rub one lime wedge around rim of glass and dip glass upside down in a saucer of salt. Refrigerate glass until ready to serve.

Put 5–6 ice cubes into cocktail shaker, then add the tequila, Cointreau and lime juice and shake. Taste. If you want it a bit sweeter, add a little granulated sugar and blend again, adding more ice if you prefer.

Pour into prepared glass. Serve with a slice of lime.

Punch with a Punch

Serves 12-16

This concoction goes back to Joan's childhood, when she drank Hawaiian Punch by the gallons. Now, of course, it has a "punch" because of the alcohol! She puts it in a huge punch bowl or spigot container when the girls come over and lets everyone serve themselves.

46 oz. pineapple juice	32 oz. ginger ale
46 oz. Hawaiian Punch	Sliced oranges, lemons, limes for garnish
½ liter bottle vodka	

Combine half the pineapple juice, Hawaiian Punch and vodka in a zip-top freezer bag; do the same with the remaining half of the ingredients. (Do not add ginger ale yet.)

Freeze to a slushy consistency, kneading occasionally.

Empty the bags into a punch bowl or container with a spigot. Add the ginger ale and citrus slices.

Kick back, put your feet up and have some punch before your guests arrive!

Pomegranate Martini

Serves 1

This is one of Joan's favorite cocktails…"feenominal," as she puts it.

2 oz. citrus vodka	Shake all ingredients well with ice and
1 oz. simple syrup or pomegranate syrup	strain into a chilled martini glass.
½ oz. fresh lemon juice	Garnish with an orange peel and serve. It's also fun to rim the glass with
¼ oz. fresh pomegranate juice	colored sugar.

This eye-popping canister is a tailor-made catchall for any A.M. recipes—simply stash 'em and cook 'em.

Rise 'n' Shine

THE BREAKFAST TIN

Even though I know I should start the day with a good breakfast, impending deadlines usually mean grabbing a cup of coffee and maybe a banana or a muffin as I crank up the computer. But weekends are different. There's plenty of time to whip up an omelet or make peach pancakes and maybe even slip a Hershey's Kiss into the filter of the coffee machine along with the ground coffee. (This is a trick I learned from a friend's husband; the chocolate melts and melds with the coffee, turning it into breakfast mocha—or as he calls it, "breakfast Mecca.") And if guests are staying over, it's an excuse to pull out all the punches with a recipe from my battered tin canister (more about that in a minute). But in the meantime, I am trying to break out of my weekday rut. Here are some goodies that do the trick; you may want to try them, too.

● **Whip up a smoothie.** Check cookbooks and the Internet for recipes, but one formula I love is to combine ½ banana with ½ cup low-fat flavored yogurt, ½ cup 1% milk, and 1 cup fresh or frozen fruit that echoes the flavor of the yogurt. Pop in a few ice cubes and pulse in a food processor until frothy.

● **Toast a frozen waffle,** then top with 1 tablespoon maple syrup, ½ cup strawberries and a little brown sugar. ➤

Veggie Quiche

85

● **Sprinkle half a grapefruit** with 1 tablespoon brown sugar and ¼ teaspoon cinnamon and pop under broiler for just a couple of minutes until the sugar caramelizes.

● **Make a tropical fruit salad** with ½ cup each of pineapple, kiwi, mango and banana chunks. Stir in a tablespoon or two of chopped walnuts and drizzle with 1 tablespoon of honey. (You also can added some shredded coconut if desired.)

● **Prepare a breakfast pizza.** Toast an English muffin, spread with melted butter and top with a mixture of cinnamon and sugar. On top of each half, put a dollop of mascarpone cheese and a tablespoon of fresh berries.

● **Nuke some cheesy eggs.** Whisk together two eggs, 1 tablespoon crumbled feta, ⅛ teaspoon each cayenne pepper, black pepper, and herbes de Provence. Pour into microwave-safe 6-oz. ramekin and cook for about 1 ½ minutes, stirring once after about 45 seconds. Remove. Cover with a paper towel, let set another minute and top with more crumbled feta, or substitute grated cheddar if you want a slightly different flavor.

THE INSPIRATION

This cheery canister is based on one I picked up at a garage sale; mine is an old Bremer's Wafers tin, slightly rusted and dinged, but the soft green color and 25-cent price tag were irresistible. It sits on my cookbook shelf holding clips and printouts for breakfasts and brunches I rarely make but always drool over. My canister does come in ➤

The Outside

The key here is a bundle of labels from breakfast products, so open the cupboard and check the fridge.

TO DO

● Find a canister to your liking—tin, glass or ceramic—wipe clean, and dry thoroughly. (If you want to change the color of your canister, coat with an appropriate paint; let dry.)

● Remove labels from tea, coffee, cereal, pancake mix, jams and jelly, maple syrup and other breakfast makings. Aim for a variety of different colors and lettering and try to locate a couple with whimsical pictures such as the little bear on the Celestial Seasonings Sleepytime Tea.
TIP When using thick labels, such as those on cardboard boxes, peel as many layers as you can from the back so label is same thickness as others.

● Attach handle of your choice with a hand drill and screws. (If canister has a neat handle already, leave as is.)

● Brush the backs of labels with matte-finish découpage glue and apply to canister in a pleasing arrangement. Wipe off any excess glue with a damp paper towel. (See Technique 101 for how to do traditional découpage.)

● Spell out words "rise and shine" with bottle-cap letters. Affix with the adhesive pads that come with the letters or use glue dots.

● Coat canister with spray-on acrylic sealer.

SPECIAL GEAR
● **Bottle-Cap Letters and Alpha Clips:** Spare Parts by The Paper Studio

TECHNIQUE 101
Classic Découpage

Originally we were going to découpage the tin, but as the process evolved, we liked the more modern look of appliquéd labels. However, if you want a traditional découpage effect, you can get it without buying any special supplies. Just check out these pointers:

1. Cut out your labels. Figure out a basic arrangement by placing labels on your tin and marking what goes where with a pencil.

2. Working with a few labels at a time, brush backs of labels with slightly diluted white glue and apply another thin layer to appropriate area of tin. Affix labels to tin, smoothing out with your fingers or a craft stick, moving outward from the center.

3. Remove excess glue with damp paper towel.

4. Repeat, overlapping labels so tin is completely covered. Let dry.

5. Now coat entire tin with more diluted white glue, taking care to smooth down every edge of every label. Let dry.

6. Apply varnish or lacquer over entire tin. Let dry. Repeat again and again until you get the patina you desire.

Start by searching around for a canister—something square or rectangular and not too large is best for this project—and you're on your way.

As easy to make as pancakes, this eye-catching tin is mostly a matter of cutting and pasting.

Let your labels be your guide to choosing the colors for your recipe cards—pick four or five predominant tones and just go for it!

GET THE LOOK

Inside the Tin

TO DO

• Select cardstock in a variety of colors (ours are earthy tones) and cut to fit box. These will become your recipe cards.

• Cut narrow bands, approximately 1 inch deep and the same width as your recipe cards from some of the cardstock. These will be your title backgrounds.

• Affix title bands about ⅜ inch down from top edges of recipe cards with a glue stick, choosing colors that contrast with each other.

• Print out recipes on plain white computer paper in the font of your choice. Cut off recipe name and affix to title bands with glue stick. Glue recipes onto other side of cards.

• Cut out or color-copy photos of recipes from books or magazines, or download and print from your computer. Glue photos of recipes onto front side of cards under recipe title.

TIP If you can't find a photo of a particular recipe, any evocative picture will do, since the recipe name is already on the card.

Banana French Toast

Veggie Quiche

A series of photo recipe cards keeps breakfast ideas at the ready.

8 Slices Raisin Bread
2 Medium bananas cut in 1/4-inch slices
1 Cup milk
4 Ounces softened cream cheese
3 Eggs
1/3 Cup sugar
3 Tablespoons all-purpose flour
2 Teaspoons vanilla extract
Powdered sugar

Heat oven to 350 F. Place four slices of raisin bread in a single layer in a buttered 9-inch square baking dish. Topwith bananas and four slices of raisin bread. Blend milk, cream cheese, eggs, sugar, flour and vanilla in a blender or food processor until smooth. POUR over raisin bread. Let stand 5 minutes or refrigerate overnight. Bake 40 to 45 minutes (50 to 55 minutes if refrigerated) until set and top is toasted. Let stand 10 minutes. Dust with powdered sugar.

1 Unbaked pie shell
2 Tbsp. Butter
1 Onion, finely chopped
2 Cloves garlic, crushed
2 cups fresh broccoli, chopped
1 Red bell pepper, diced
1 Green bell pepper, diced
1 1/2 cups grated cheese
4 Eggs, well beaten
1 1/2 cups Milk
Salt and pepper to taste

Preheat oven 350 degrees F. In large saucepan over medium heat melt butter and saute onion, garlic, broccoli and peppers until tender. Spoon vegetables into pie crust and sprinkle with cheese. Set aside.

In a large mixing bowl, throughly combine eggs and milk and season with salt and pepper. Pour egg mixture over vegetables into pie crust. Cook for about 30 minutes, or until knife comes out clean.

handy, though, whenever guests are staying for the weekend—it's the perfect opportunity for an indulgent brunch with friends. Sometimes I pull out the recipe for Ham and Cheese Biscuits (always a winner), another time I'll choose Huevos Rancheros (I have a half-dozen versions of this), and if I'm feeling really energized I'll go for Lee Bailey's Chili-Tomato Eggs in Bread Crumb Cups.

One Saturday, staring at the tin itself, I had an "aha" moment. The tin was an ideal vehicle for *Cookbooking*. We could take any plain canister and découpage it with a jumble of breakfast labels or other kitchen-inspired icons. Cooks could coordinate the cutouts to their décor, display the canister in a choice place, and if they were so inspired, slick up their mishmash of recipes by gluing them onto pieces of cardstock.

FYI: In the process of putting this project together, we took a shortcut: Instead of doing traditional découpage, we simply glued the labels onto the surface, then finished off with a spray-on sealant. Easy. Quick. Smart. ■ ■ ■

GET THE LOOK
Finishing Touches

Imaginative alphabet clips add a fanciful touch to the cards. We spelled out the word "yummy," but you could be more of a purist and categorize your recipes by letter: E for eggs, P for pancakes and so on.

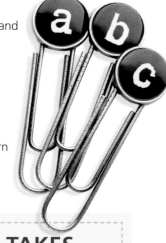

TO DO

● Attach alphabet clips to cards in a staggered pattern to spell out the word of your choice.

DIFFERENT TAKES

Check out the kitchen department of your local home center for cabinet handles based on flatware. A specially-shaped spoon or knife would make a great topper for your tin. Or match the handle to the hardware on your kitchen cabinets.

Make it easy on yourself: Forgo the photos altogether and simply glue recipe printouts or clippings onto the cards.

We like the look of breakfast labels, but you could employ any kind of cutouts: cartoons of food scenes, pictures of barnyard animals, even snippets of family photos. Or, think pattern-on-pattern and use fabric remnants in stripes, checks and dots for a bright patchwork look. Different bandanna swatches would also work. Just remember, if you use fabric, choose a specially formulated fabric glue.

Recipes to Try

Huevos Rancheros

Serves 4

● You'll need a few pots for this, but the steps are easy and the results memorable. For a refreshing tweak, top with slices of fresh avocado. For something spicier and heartier, brown some chopped chorizo in a skillet and place on the eggs before adding the salsa.

2 teaspoons vegetable oil

4 large corn tortillas

2 tablespoons unsalted butter

8 large eggs

1½ cups grated Monterey Jack or taco cheese

1 cup refried beans, warmed

1 cup salsa, warmed

In a large skillet, heat ½ teaspoon of the vegetable oil over medium-high heat. Add 1 tortilla and cook until warmed through and just starting to brown. Flip and cook on other side. Remove, place on platter and cover with towel. Repeat with remaining tortillas and oil.

In a large skillet, melt the butter over medium-high heat. Break eggs into skillet and fry until slightly runny, just about 1 minute. Sprinkle with cheese and cover for approximately another 1½ minutes, until eggs are finished cooking and cheese is melted. (You can also do this in two skillets if you don't have one large enough to hold 8 eggs.)

Place a warm tortilla on a plate and spread with about 2 tablespoons of warm refried beans. Place 2 eggs on top of beans and top with 2 tablespoons of the warmed salsa.

Serve immediately.

French Toast with Baked Bananas

Serves 4

● A luscious weekend treat that's especially tasty served with a mixture of fresh berries. Kids, however, seem to love this with lots of real maple syrup.

4 large eggs	4 bananas, peeled
½ cup milk	2 tablespoons fresh lemon juice
1 tablespoon sugar	4 tablespoons butter, (2 cut into small pieces)
½ teaspoon vanilla extract	
1 teaspoon ground cinnamon	2 tablespoons brown sugar
4 thick slices brioche or challah bread	Powdered sugar (optional)

Preheat oven to 350 degrees F.

Beat the eggs, milk, sugar, vanilla and a couple of pinches of cinnamon together in a mixing bowl until well blended. Pour the egg mixture into a large baking pan, one big enough to hold all the bread.

Lay the bread slices in the egg mixture and let them soak, turning gently several times, until the bread has absorbed all the egg.

While bread is soaking, slice 4 bananas in half lengthwise. Sprinkle with lemon juice, then top with the pieces of butter, the brown sugar and the remaining cinnamon. Bake for about 10 minutes, or until golden.

In the meantime, heat the remaining 2 tablespoons butter in a large, nonstick skillet over medium-low heat. When the butter starts to bubble, lay the soaked bread in the pan. Cook, turning once, until the bread is nicely browned and cooked through, about 12 minutes.

To serve, place two slices of banana over each slice of toast; top with powdered sugar if desired.

To Your Health

THE FIT FILE

These days even the most sedentary person is aware of the connection between fitness and health, and almost everyone knows someone who runs. I did it myself years ago, teaming up with my friend Jean a few evenings a week. We'd meet on the Upper East Side of Manhattan where we both lived, and run along the East River. Or should I say *attempt* to run? Even though we were diligent about warming up and did flexibility exercises on alternate days, the clump-clump-clump along the city pavement seemed especially grueling. Inevitably one of us would cry uncle, and we'd limp over to a local restaurant and dive into carbs we didn't need.

After six months we called it quits. Jean joined a gym; I started taking yoga classes. But running is still America's number one fitness choice and those who do it swear by it, citing more energy, better stamina and increased well-being.

Gloria Tracy is one of those people, and her story is particularly inspiring. Once upon a time she was your stereotypical klutzy kid—the one who wore thick eyeglasses and was always last to be chosen for any team. Even as an adult she felt awkward and steered away from anything physical. "The only thing I was coordinated at ➤

Even the back cover sends a positive, uplifting message.

Funky yarns and felt geometrics make this "fit file" all the more fun to use.

93

was crafting," she laughs. "I could sew and knit and bead along with the best of them. But swinging a bat or doing a sprint—forget it!"

Fast-forward to 2008. Gloria has completed several marathons and runs four days a week. The turning point was in 2001, when her adult son received a diagnosis of stage-four colon cancer. "As a mom I wanted to take some kind of action, to do something that would help," she says. An acquaintance suggested running a marathon to promote the fight against cancer. "Who, me? No way," Gloria remembers. But the thought resonated, and she began training and working with a nutritionist. Slowly but surely she changed her diet, reshaped her body and built up her stamina.

"My initial reason for running was to raise funds for cancer research, and I will continue to do that, but along the way I've discovered a strength and power I never knew I had," she says. ➤

GET THE LOOK
The Cover

When Gloria first conceived of this project, two things were firm in her mind: "I wanted it to be tall and skinny to symbolize a lean, fit body, and I wanted it to color-coordinate with my running gear." Check out Gloria's photo and you'll see that the palette does indeed synchronize with her workout clothes.

TO DO

- Select a narrow album, (ours is approximately 13 ½" x 6 ½") and make three holes in both back and front spines with a hand drill. Thread three 1 ½" metal rings through holes to attach front and back covers.

- Drill three more holes along top edge of front cover; attach three 1" metal rings.

- Cut two pieces self-adhesive felt in black and white to fit front cover, making the black one just a bit bigger to achieve a more interesting effect. Affix in place, leaving the spine bare.

- Sketch out title ("Run Fast, Eat Good Food") with a pencil, aiming for a freeform lettering effect. (Note: Gloria ran the title vertically so she could stand the book up on her kitchen counter.)

- Choose a fuzzy teal and a smoother lavender yarn (or any yarns of your choice) and affix over the lettering using a glue stick.

- Finish by gluing on a large button near the bottom edge. (Since the last word on this book is "food" Gloria used her button to stand in for the letter "o".)

- Adorn spine with more stickers and small felt pieces.

- For the back cover, affix some scrapbook sayings and affirmations. For visual impact, choose a mix of shapes, textures, colors.

- Glue a small elastic loop at bottom edge of back cover, checking that it will fit over the button on the front cover.

Embellish with a strand of tiny beads, pieces of ribbon, yarn and felt, cut into shapes of your choice and any small stickers you may desire (Gloria picked dots).

The choice of materials—yarn, felt, beads—speaks to Gloria's love of texture.

"I feel confident and able to take on the world. Whether or not my running has had anything to do with John's survival, I'll never know. Seven years later though, he's OK—that's a powerful motivator."

Gloria also turns to her personally designed journal for encouragement. "I needed a guide to help myself stay on track, but I couldn't find anything that inspired me, so I put on my crafter's hat and produced my own." The album's bohemian style gives no clue to the efficiency within. Gloria's book offers space for tucking notes, a chart for tracking workouts, photos for inspiration, even nifty pockets for attitude adjusters. Although created for a runner, it can be tweaked to suit any fitness personality. For instance, you could convert the runner's log into a gym journal where you can record your different workouts and how you felt afterward. So look at Gloria's book as a prototype that you can transform into something uniquely yours.

THE INSPIRATION

It goes without saying that this isn't your typical runner's journal. Fluffy fibers, tiny beads and one-of-a-kind lettering all testify to a crafter's touch. "The crafting thing is innate with me," Gloria states. "I grew up in the Midwest in a household where sewing and pasting and making things were parts of daily life. I was always designing something—a centerpiece, a scrapbook or a project for 4-H."

As a partner in a firm that develops products ➤

The Inside Covers

As a designer, Gloria knows this is prime space, and she's used it well, creating pockets to store important info.

TO DO

● Cut a plastic pocket to fit onto inside of front cover. Affix with glue stick. This where Gloria keeps her runner's log.

● Suspend a sectioned plastic page from the three rings so it hangs over the pocket. Again, you may have to cut to size. This is where Gloria puts her current food intake, recorded on small color-coded slips of paper.

● Affix another plastic pocket to inside back cover with a glue stick.

● Attach plastic words and sayings such as "control your destiny" on insides of both front and back covers. **TIP** Check out the scrapbooking section of your local craft store to find phrases to your liking.

The Binder

TO DO

● Select a plastic loose-leaf binder that will fit album. Attach a 3½" strip of ¾"-wide Velcro about halfway down front cover at right edge; add another strip to back cover of album, checking placement to make sure the binder fits and will stay in place. (Note: The binder fits vertically into the album.)

● Affix self-adhesive letters onto colored self-adhesive dots to spell out the title for the binder. (Ours says "Gloria's Food Guide.") Affix to a small strip of paper and cut to size to fit along the spine of the binder.

● Decorate cover page of binder with photos and words of your choice.

● Find a small plastic envelope; adorn with stick-on word "attitude" and fill with pieces of paper on which you can write affirmations. Fasten to binder pocket with colored paper clip.

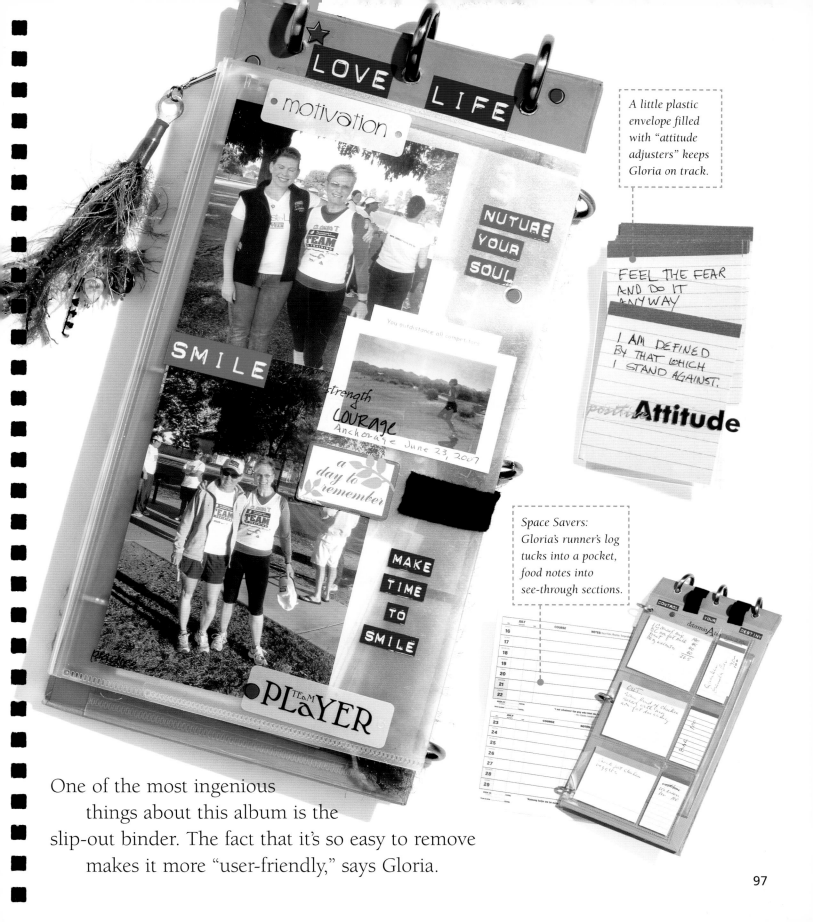

LOVE LIFE

motivation

NUTURE YOUR SOUL

SMILE

strength
COURAGE
Anchorage June 23, 2007

a day to remember

You outdistance all competitors

MAKE TIME TO SMILE

TEAM PLAYER

A little plastic envelope filled with "attitude adjusters" keeps Gloria on track.

FEEL THE FEAR AND DO IT ANYWAY

I AM DEFINED BY THAT WHICH I STAND AGAINST.

positive Attitude

Space Savers: Gloria's runner's log tucks into a pocket, food notes into see-through sections.

CONTROL YOUR DESTINY

determine Attitude

One of the most ingenious things about this album is the slip-out binder. The fact that it's so easy to remove makes it more "user-friendly," says Gloria.

for the knitting and hobby industry, Gloria is still designing. "But running has become as integral to my life as knitting and gluing. I now pay as much attention to calorie intake and output as I do to choosing yarn, and I count carbs with the same dedication that I count stitches," she explains. "This album plays to my imaginative self, but is actually very practical, exactly what I need to stay disciplined."

You can see what Gloria means when you go through the book. On the inside of the front cover is her running log, slipped into a plastic pocket. A separate multipocketed sleeve holds slips of paper where she jots down a particular day's food intake. "The papers are so tiny I can carry them with me and write down what I eat immediately. That way I never goof up."

Just as handy is the other part of the book: a narrow plastic binder that acts as Gloria's food diary and also displays photos, affirmations and nutrition tips. "This attaches to the album with a piece of Velcro so that I can slip it out whenever I want to review my progress or add new items," she explains.

"I'm pleased with the way this turned out," she continues. "It reflects both Glorias—the artist and the athlete." ■ ■ ■

GET THE LOOK
The Dividers

TO DO

● Cut colored plastic sheets in staggered sizes to act as dividers and label with categories of your choice using self-adhesive dots and letters. Trim outer edges of dividers with stitching. (See Technique 101.)

SPECIAL GEAR
● **Self-adhesive felt:** Fiber Tack

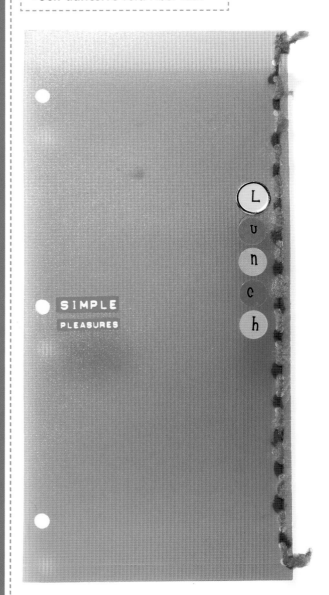

RELAXATION

TECHNIQUE 101
A Stitch in Time

The divider's stitched edges echo the texture play on the front cover and reflect Gloria's crafty personality.

Use a single-hole punch to make a series of small holes ¼" apart along outer edges of dividers.

Choose different yarns or narrow ribbon to contrast with the colors of the dividers. Stitch through the holes with a knitting needle, using a variety of stitches.

Knot at ends; trim edges.

Jazz up dividers with simple words like "relaxation" or "energy"— anything that is meaningful to you.

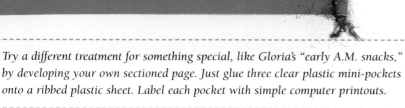

Try a different treatment for something special, like Gloria's "early A.M. snacks," by developing your own sectioned page. Just glue three clear plastic mini-pockets onto a ribbed plastic sheet. Label each pocket with simple computer printouts.

The Pages

TO DO

- Select sectioned plastic pages to file handwritten notes and logs. Gloria used ones with three and five sections to fit store-bought notepapers.

- Create a special tips page by slipping computer printouts into each sectioned slot. Gloria concentrated on The Big Four nutrition tips, but this could include weight-loss strategies, mental exercises or workout guidelines.

Finishing Touches

TO DO

- Make a tassel using a tassel tool and various yarns and fibers; add beads and attach to a clasp or ring.

DIFFERENT TAKES

An easy but effective alternative for the cover title is to use ribbon, twine or string instead of yarn. Braid, if it is narrow enough, also works well.

Embellish edges of dividers with strips of patterned or solid paper or fabric. Use decorative shears to cut and adhere with a glue stick.

Create your own personal affirmations by stamping or hand-lettering words onto pieces of colored construction paper. Affix to pages with a glue stick.

live your dream

Recipes to Try

Pepper Medley

Serves 2

● This dish is a staple of Gloria's diet—tasty on its own, served with sautéed shrimp or chicken for a protein boost, or alongside steamed white or brown rice or pasta for a carb hit.

1 tablespoon olive or canola oil

1 garlic clove, peeled and chopped

2 bell peppers, 1 red and 1 orange or yellow, chopped into small pieces

1 handful of grape tomatoes

Pinch of sugar

Salt and pepper to taste

Heat oil in skillet on medium and add garlic; sauté about 30 seconds.

Add peppers, sugar and salt and pepper to taste. Saute 4 or 5 minutes or until peppers become tender. Toss in tomatoes and cook another 3 minutes.

Cover, turn off heat and let stand another few minutes so flavors meld.

Serve on its own as a veggie dish, or with additions (see above) as an entrée.

Eating right just got easier. Try these special faves from Gloria.

Fruit Slushy

Serves 1

● This drink is a runner's dream, providing protein, carbs and fiber. The recipe is so foolproof, you can vary the ingredients to create exactly the flavor you want. Diet orange soda, for instance, makes a lush orange slushy similar to a Creamsicle. Gloria usually starts her day off with one version or another; she also likes to whip up a small glass for a snack.

1 can diet lemon/lime soda

Nonfat cottage cheese

Nonfat yogurt

¼–½ cup frozen fruit

Artificial sweetener, if desired

Depending upon how large a drink you want, you can use ¼, ⅓ or ½ cup each of the cottage cheese and yogurt. You can also use any kind of frozen fruit, or a mix.

Put soda in blender first, then cottage cheese and yogurt, and lastly the frozen fruit. Blend until fruit is slushy. If it is too thick, add cold water or nonfat milk.

The calories vary as follows:

¼ cup each of the cottage cheese and yogurt and three or four strawberries or ¼ cup frozen fruit will be about 85 calories of *yum!*

⅓ cup each of the cottage cheese and yogurt and ¼ cup of frozen fruit will be about 125 calories of *yum! yum!*

½ cup each of the cottage cheese and yogurt and ½ cup of frozen fruit will be about 170 calories of *yum! yum! yum!*

Thrills from the Grill

THE GRILL BOARD

We're a nation of grillers. Folks in warmer regions spend a much of their cooking time on decks and patios with state-of-the-art equipment; people in northern states so hunger for the taste of fire and smoke, they put on big, puffy parkas and stand in the snow, grilling up burgers and steaks.

In my neck of the woods in southern New England, you can catch the tantalizing whiff of barbecue as early as March, when daylight begins to linger longer. I always look forward to a spring fête with my friends Lindsay and Tom, knowing Tom will be outside, rain or shine, grilling something fabulous. He has an uncanny ability to predict when food is done, always delivering the most succulent scallops, the tenderest corn, the flakiest fish. Unlike some men, Tom also cooks indoors—he even bakes bread!—so the women at the party can never accuse him of giving in to "a boy thing." But when pressed, he admits to the macho pull of the grill, saying there is something sexier about stoking the coals than standing at the stove.

While I may be more comfortable in the kitchen, I, too, often succumb to the thrill of the grill. Grilled food does taste different—the slight charring, the hint of smokiness, the way ➤

➤

GET THE LOOK
The Cover

TO DO

- Purchase a shiny metal clipboard in the size of your choice.

- Select a red metallic scrapbook paper and cut to approximately one-third the size of the clipboard in order to reveal the pages beneath. (Ours measures 8½" x 5" to coordinate with a 9" x 12½" clipboard.)

- Create the curved corners with a corner punch.

- Trace letters from an alphabet stencil onto black construction paper. Adhere with a glue stick.

Who knew a clipboard could look so neat—and serve such a purpose? It's the ideal vehicle for red, black and silver cookbook pages.

Simple as can be, the title page of this book is flashy red metallic emblazoned with the words "Scott's Grill" in big black letters. Definitely something a guy will appreciate!

Staggering the sizes of the papers allows easy access to all your recipes.

SCOTT'S GRILL
MEAT
POULTRY
VEGGIES
SEAFOOD

Our grill board has a no-frills, industrial look—cool, hip and just masculine enough to get him fired up.

103

flavors of certain ingredients intensify as others mellow. But it was with Tom in mind, not my own grilling habits, that the idea of a grill clipboard came into being. One rainy night, barbecue tongs in hand, he walked over to the rest of us with some sauce-stained printouts in hand, complaining that the recipe instructions were too blurred to read. Poor guy, I thought, he needs wipe-clean recipe cards. Bingo! Why not *cookbook* a series of laminated pages and attach them to a very modern, very manly stainless-steel clipboard, complete with a loop to hang on the grill? If it had a hip industrial look, a man wouldn't be embarrassed to use it. Thus, our Grill Board was born.

THE INSPIRATION

Although we wanted this design to have a masculine feel, it's not too testosterone-heavy. The sleek, streamlined look and black, red and silver palette appeal to both sexes. Best of all, it's easy to put together and the laminated pages wipe clean in an instant. Our test panel of three guys— Tom, Scott and John—gave it a thumbs-up, and even passed along some of their own tried-and-true grilling basics:

● "I always bank my briquettes so there's an area that's free of coals," says Tom. "This way I can shift food around to prevent burning, or cook certain items over indirect heat, others on a high flame."

● Tom cautions about piercing or constantly lifting food off the grill to check for doneness. "Leave it be for the recommended cooking time, then remove with tongs or a spatula. ➤

The Dividers

TO DO

● Select 12" x 12" papers: We used "wrinkled" black and silver and matte red along with a speckled paper we created just for the fun of it.

● Since the dividers need to be different sizes in order to reveal the category names, stack in the order they will appear. Mark the appropriate lengths for each with a pencil.

● Cut dividers to size, snipping the corners into a slightly curved shape with a corner punch.

● Fill in category names using an alphabet stencil and different colored paint pens. Remember to lift stencil immediately after filling in to prevent blurred edges. **TIP** For an easier approach, use stick-on stencil letters.

● To create the gray-and-white granite paper, apply a textured spray paint to cardstock, let dry and cut to size. (See Technique 101.)

● Stencil on title.

SPECIAL GEAR
● **Wrinkled papers:** ProvoCraft
● **Paint pens:** Krylon
● **Speckled granite look spray paint:** "Stone" by Krylon

TECHNIQUE 101

Texture Play
Our nifty "granite" paper is more a strategy than a technique, but it's well worth trying.

Select a spray-on textured paint specially formulated for use on paper. Suede, leather and stone finishes are available in a range of tones.

Lay sheet of cardstock on surface covered with newspaper.

Spray lightly, moving can back and forth horizontally; let dry several hours or overnight. Add another coat if you desire a thicker texture. (Some manufacturers suggest using a clear sealant, but it's not necessary for this application.)

Too much poking releases necessary juices and causes a loss of flavor."

● To make cleanup easier and prevent foods from sticking, Scott lightly coats the grate with oil before he's ready to cook. You can either brush on vegetable or olive oil (depending on the food) or pour a small amount of oil onto a cloth and just wipe on.

● John, who likes to marinate meat and poultry in all sorts of concoctions, offers this tip: "Make sure your food is almost dry when you place it on the grill—too wet and you'll have a mess. Pat with a paper towel to remove excess, and brush with marinade as it's cooking."

● John's newest technique is to grill fish, especially salmon, on a cedar plank. To do, soak the plank in salted water for at least an hour, then place the plank directly on the grill over medium-high heat. Sometimes John simply seasons the fish with salt and pepper, other times he coats it with a mustard or lemon-oil glaze. Either way, he swears by the smokey taste the cedar delivers.

● And this last guideline from Tom: "Always have water nearby. I keep a filled watering can next to the grill, but a spray bottle works just as well. Believe me, it comes in handy." ■ ■ ■

The Pages

Once again, the look is clean and streamlined.

TO DO

● Cut black scrapbook paper to size, coordinating with the appropriate dividers. (We were able to find subtly pinstriped black paper, but solid is fine.)

● Print recipes on plain white computer paper, cut to size and affix to black paper with an ordinary stapler. (If desired, add pictures or illustrations to recipes.)

● Laminate recipe pages at a local copy center.

● Place pages in desired order and attach to clipboard.

Finishing Touches

A loop of braided leather makes theclipboard easy to attach to the grill.

TO DO

● Nothing to it—just purchase a length of leather in the jewelry section of the crafts store. Twine would also work, but the leather has a classier effect.

DIFFERENT TAKES

A clear Lucite or solid black plastic clipboard are neat alternatives to a metal one. They're just as easy to wipe clean, and they have a crisp, modern look.

For a more folksy palette, experiment with papers in denim and bandanna patterns for the dividers and back the recipes with a blue and white ticking print. Or, create a series of faux-suede dividers in earthy tones of caramel, tan, and brown by using textured paints.

Instead of stenciling the titles, try stamping. Or, forgo lettering altogether and use icons such as a chicken, cow, fish, etc., to indicate the categories.

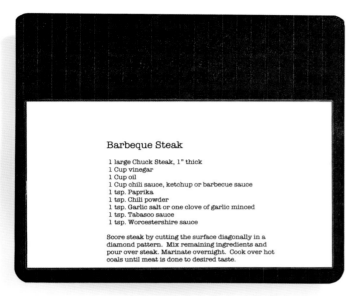

Barbeque Steak

1 large Chuck Steak, 1" thick
1 Cup vinegar
1 Cup oil
1 Cup chili sauce, ketchup or barbecue sauce
1 tsp. Paprika
1 tsp. Chili powder
1 tsp. Garlic salt or one clove of garlic minced
1 tsp. Tabasco sauce
1 tsp. Worcestershire sauce

Score steak by cutting the surface diagonally in a diamond pattern. Mix remaining ingredients and pour over steak. Marinate overnight. Cook over hot coals until meat is done to desired taste.

Grilled Chicken

Bone and skin a bunch of chicken thighs and then sprinkle a packet of Emeril's BAM spice packet over. Meanwhile get the grill going and when the coals are hot spread out the coals good so you are more or less cooking over indirect heat.

Put the thighs on the grill and continuously turn them, spraying or basting with beer after every turn. It won't take them long to cook and they are SO GOOD!

Easy Grill Potatoes & Veggies

4- large baking potatoes
4- carrots
1-large or 2 medium onions
Butter or bacon grease

Wash potatoes and carrots, slice 1/4 inch thick crosswise. Peel and slice the onions. Season with salt, pepper, and seasoning salt. For spicy spuds, sprinkle with chili powder. Dot with several chunks of butter or a couple teaspoons of bacon grease. Wrap in aluminum foil to make a packet, wrap a second time in the opposite direction to seal packet. Place on grill and let cook for about 20 minutes. Open carefully as they are hot and steamy fresh off the grill. They are really great with a nice thick steak.

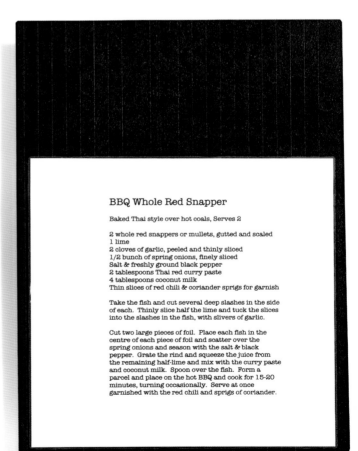

BBQ Whole Red Snapper

Baked Thai style over hot coals, Serves 2

2 whole red snappers or mullets, gutted and scaled
1 lime
2 cloves of garlic, peeled and thinly sliced
1/2 bunch of spring onions, finely sliced
Salt & freshly ground black pepper
2 tablespoons Thai red curry paste
4 tablespoons coconut milk
Thin slices of red chili & coriander sprigs for garnish

Take the fish and cut several deep slashes in the side of each. Thinly slice half the lime and tuck the slices into the slashes in the fish, with slivers of garlic.

Cut two large pieces of foil. Place each fish in the centre of each piece of foil and scatter over the spring onions and season with the salt & black pepper. Grate the rind and squeeze the juice from the remaining half-lime and mix with the curry paste and coconut milk. Spoon over the fish. Form a parcel and place on the hot BBQ and cook for 15-20 minutes, turning occasionally. Serve at once garnished with the red chili and sprigs of coriander.

No BBQ sauce on these pages!
Get them laminated at a copy center.

Recipes to Try

Just about everything—even dessert—tastes better grilled.

Asian Grilled Swordfish

Serves 4

● My friend Gina makes this dish over and over again during the summer, sometimes substituting another thick meaty fish for the swordfish. For accompaniments that are just as simple to put together, try a vegetable cous-cous or rice pilaf and a tossed salad with sliced oranges and toasted almonds.

2 tablespoons soy sauce

2 tablespoons orange juice

1 tablespoon tomato paste

1 tablespoon parsley

1 clove of garlic, minced

½ teaspoon lemon juice

½ teaspoon dried oregano

½ teaspoon freshly ground black pepper

4 swordfish steaks, about 1½ lbs total

Mix all ingredients except for swordfish together. Place swordfish steaks in glass baking dish and cover with marinade, turning fish several times to coat well. Cover and refrigerate for at least an hour, longer if possible.

When ready to grill, remove swordfish from marinade and pat slightly dry before you place on grate. Grill approximately 4 minutes on each side.

Hot Buttered Rum Nectarines

Serves 9

● A couple of years ago I starting grilling fruit and I've been like a little kid ever since, experimenting with pineapples, peaches, plums, bananas, you name it. These nectarines, slathered with sweet rum and butter mixture are divine on their own, but even better served with a dollop of vanilla ice cream or sweetened mascarpone. If you can't find nectarines, substitute peaches.

6 firm nectarines, halved and pitted

¼ cup rum

¼ cup melted butter

¼ cup brown sugar

½ teaspoon cinnamon

½ teaspoon ground ginger

½ teaspoon nutmeg

Combine the rum and melted butter and add the brown sugar, stirring until it dissolves.

Add the spices and stir to combine thoroughly.

Brush the nectarine halves on each side with the spice mixture and let stand at room temperature for 5 minutes to absorb the buttered rum.

Grill on medium heat for about 10 minutes, basting with the spice mixture and turning occasionally. Nectarines are done when golden brown. Let cool 1-2 minutes, then serve. Or place in a glass baking dish and keep warm in oven till ready.

Rosemary Mustard Pork Tenderloins

Serves 6

● Another treat from Gina, these pork tenderloins are easy to pop on the grill and a nice change from chicken. If you want more of a kick, add a few drops of hot sauce to the marinade.

3 tablespoons olive oil

½ cup Dijon-style mustard

3 cloves garlic, minced

½ tablespoon fresh rosemary, finely chopped

1 teaspoon Worcestershire sauce

Freshly ground pepper, to taste

2 pork tenderloins, about 1-lb each

Blend all ingredients except for the pork together with a whisk. Place pork in plastic resealable bag and add marinade, squishing around to make sure meat is well covered. Place in refrigerator for several hours.

One hour before grilling remove marinated meat from refrigerator to bring to room temperature.

Coat grill with olive oil to prevent meat from sticking. Grill pork, turning several times, for approximately 20-25 minutes.

Saucy Apricot Chicken Serves 6

● This is a variation on my mother's apricot glazed Cornish hens that I've been making since I was a teenager. The soy sauce and garlic cut the sweetness of the apricot jam just enough.

1 cup apricot jam

2 tablespoons lemon juice

1 tablespoon apricot nectar

1 tablespoon soy sauce

1 garlic clove, minced

Kosher salt and pepper to taste

6 chicken cutlets, pounded to ¼-inch thick

6 canned apricots, halved

Vegetable oil

Mix the jam, lemon juice, apricot nectar and soy sauce in a bowl. Add minced garlic, salt and pepper and blend well.

Preheat grill until coals are glowing and hot. Place chicken on lightly oiled grate and brush with one-third of the glaze. Grill about 3 minutes. Flip over and brush with another third of the glaze. Grill about 3 minutes more. (Test for doneness by lightly nicking with a knife: The inside should be white but still moist.) Transfer to a platter and cover with aluminum foil to retain heat.

Meanwhile, heat the remaining glaze.

Brush apricots with vegetable oil and place on grill, cut sides down. Cook for about 1 to 1½ minutes on each side. Place over the cutlets, then drizzle cutlets with remaining heated glaze. *Note: You can also prepare the cutlets and apricots on a stovetop grill pan, or pan-grill them in a skillet. Keep warm by covering with foil or placing in a 250 degree oven.*

Herbed Shrimp

Serves 6

○ This dish takes just minutes to prep; you'll spend the most time mincing the different herbs!

2 lbs. large easy-peel shrimp (16 to 20 per pound), shelled but with tails left on

3 cloves garlic, minced

2 shallots, diced

1 garlic clove, diced

Pinch of red pepper flakes

¼ cup fresh parsley, minced

¼ cup fresh basil, minced

⅛ cup fresh thyme, minced

2 teaspoons Dijon-style mustard

2 teaspoons kosher salt

½ teaspoon freshly ground black pepper

½ cup extra-virgin olive oil

1 lemon, juiced

36 cherry tomatoes

Olive oil for brushing tomatoes

Combine all the ingredients except the tomatoes and olive oil and allow to marinate for 1 hour at room temperature, or cover and refrigerate overnight.

Preheat the grill, brushing the grate with oil to prevent shrimp from sticking.

While grill is heating, soak 12 bamboo skewers in water.

Brush the cherry tomatoes lightly with olive oil.

Thread 3 shrimp and 3 tomatoes on each skewer. Grill for about 1½ minutes on each side. Serve immediately.
Note: The shrimp can also be done on a grill pan on top of the stove or placed under the broiler for approximately 3 minutes.

*Iain's clan tartan was the inspiration for this
cover—the perfect background for the family crest.*

Family Heirlooms

THE HERITAGE ALBUM

When most of us think about heirlooms, we picture things like well-loved china, slightly chipped and faded; a wedding dress, carefully folded and covered with tissue; quilts, perhaps a bit threadbare, that have kept friends and family warm. Furniture, rugs, photos and jewelry also make the list. But recipes are heirlooms, too: compelling links to those who lived years ago. While we may not cook meals in the same way, these slips of paper—'receipts' as they used to be called—give us a glimpse of family life as it used to be.

I cherish a recipe for chicken fricassee with dumplings that my father's mother used to make. She brought up seven boys and one girl in a five-room apartment in an area of Manhattan called Hell's Kitchen. I still recall the wonder of visiting this place as a small child, walking into the huge dining room, my grandfather rocking in his favorite chair, my grandmother bustling about in a long narrow kitchen with a sink as large as a bathtub. (As a toddler, I was bathed in that sink.) Tantalizing aromas would greet my parents and me and we would all sit around the scarred wooden table, primed to dig into any number of dishes. Grandma always prepared the chicken because I was a finicky eater and she knew just what I liked. I loved the oh-so-tender pieces ➤

of meat dripping with a buttery sauce, and—even more—the weirdly shaped dumplings, plump and eggy and just chewy enough. To this day, it's a dish I prepare when I don't feel well: the ultimate comfort food, conjured up with love, memories and homemade chicken stock.

Although I rely on a few other dishes from Grandma's repertoire, I haven't been as lucky as my friend Iain Hunter, caretaker of a veritable treasure trove of family recipes from Scotland and England. There's the Hunter family shortbread, salmon mousse, orange fool, Elizabethan pork. Oddly enough, all these cherished recipes, written in tiny handwriting on small slips of paper, were stashed in a tattered manila folder—not at all like Iain, who's usually extremely organized and very meticulous. "I've been meaning to do something with these," he mumbles when I comment on the sorry state of the folder. "I bring them with me wherever I live (Hong Kong, Australia, New York) but I've never gotten around to doing them up right." What a beginning for a heritage album! Combined with family lore, age-old photos and Scottish poems, we have a mother lode of material for a *Cookbooking* project.

As personal and unique as Iain's album may be, it will inspire you to create your own ➤

GET THE LOOK
The Cover

TO DO

- Start with a 12" x 12" post-bound book in a rich green faux leather.

- Cut a square of tartan fabric just a bit smaller than the cover, about 10 ½" x 10 ½". Pull threads at edges to create a slight fringe. Center fabric on cover and affix with glue stick.

- Scan and print out crest or take to a copy center to reproduce.

- Select a piece of cardstock in a finish of your choice (we chose woodgrain) and center the crest on top of it; sketch a shield shape onto the cardstock to create a "mat" for the crest. Check positioning, affix crest to cardstock with glue stick and cut along your sketch lines.

TIP A simple circle or square or diamond would work equally well, but the shield form has an interesting old-world touch.

- Place the matted crest on top of piece of black faux leather and sketch out a larger shield shape to act as a frame. (See template.) Cut out leather shield. Affix crest to leather shield with fabric glue.

- Cut a 10 ½" x 2" strip of the black faux leather and topstitch top and bottom edges. Affix near bottom edge of tartan, about 1" from edge, with fabric glue.

- Center shield with the crest inside on the tartan fabric, making sure bottom point goes over horizontal leather band. Affix with fabric glue.

- Finish off by affixing a faux or dried sprig of thistle, pine or berries at the upper left corner.

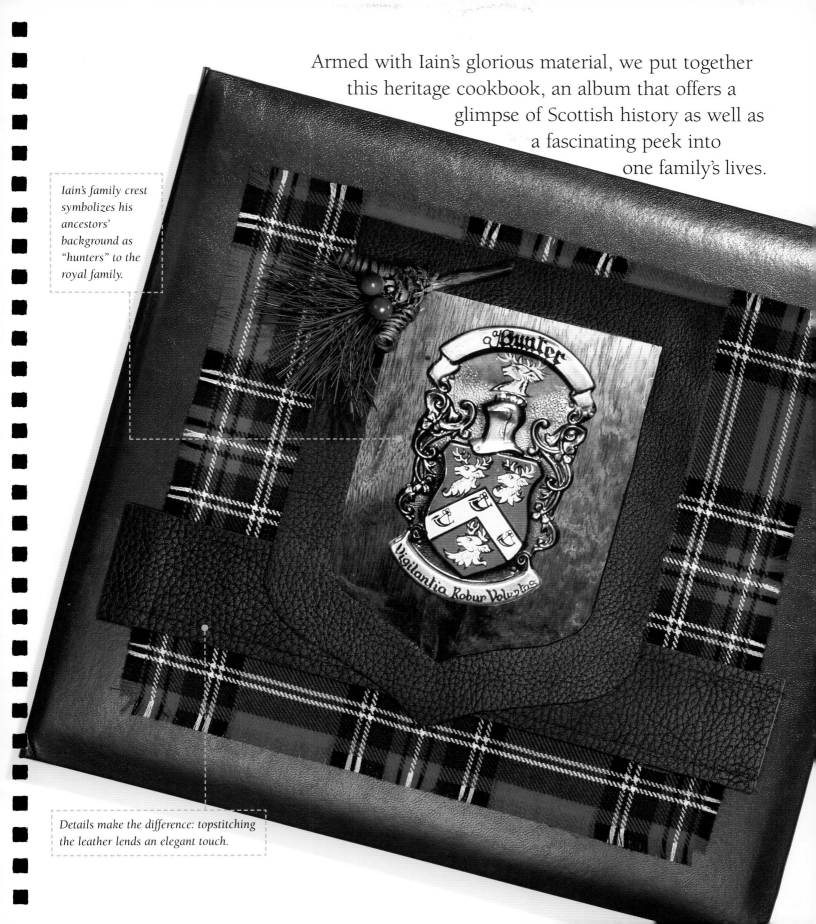

Armed with Iain's glorious material, we put together this heritage cookbook, an album that offers a glimpse of Scottish history as well as a fascinating peek into one family's lives.

Iain's family crest symbolizes his ancestors' background as "hunters" to the royal family.

Details make the difference: topstitching the leather lends an elegant touch.

The Endpapers

TO DO

- Start by gluing green construction paper over both inside covers to provide a rich background for your chosen art. (If inside cover is already the color of your choice, you can skip this step).

- Color copy a map of your homeland (in this case Scotland) to the green paper with a glue stick.

- Arrange family photos, recipes, and any other ephemera in a pleasing arrangement on the map.

- Embellish with paper and metal frames and photo corners. Affix into place with glue dots or a glue stick. (Since the recipes will be on the following pages, we only used one for each of the endpapers).

The inside covers are an evocative assemblage of family
photos, recipes and other appropriate ephemera.

GET THE LOOK
Frontispiece

A dramatic frontispiece with the family name spelled out in leather echoes the mood of the cover.

TO DO

●For the frontispiece: Cut faux black leather into a 12" x 12" square and punch holes to match up with the posts of the scrapbook.

●Center a slightly smaller square of tartan on the leather and affix with spray adhesive.

●Cut a wide strip of the faux leather to fit over the tartan and affix with fabric glue. Using a stencil, draw out letters of the family name onto another piece of

the faux leather, cut with a fabric knife and affix to the leather strip with the suede side up.

●Adorn with a small metal frame affixed with rubber cement on top. We placed a traditional Scottish pin in the center.

●Add a mini-book of Scottish poems hung from thin black ribbon from the corner of the page. (See Technique 101, page 121.)

GET THE LOOK
Back Page

The back page, marked by Iain's Scottish pins and a Robert Burns poem, provides a sentimental closure.

TO DO

• Center square of tartan fabric to green scrapbook page as explained previously.

• Affix selected pages from old Scottish books or other publications atop the fabric. (Iain had some lovely poems and Scottish landscape scenes, so we were

lucky, but such ephemera can usually be found at flea markets.)

• For texture, add something three-dimensional. We attached Iain's kilt and crest pins to a folded piece of fabric placed in a paper frame.

heirloom, something to enjoy now and keep for generations to come.

THE INSPIRATION

Being invited to dinner at my friend Iain's is a wonderful treat. This man can tell a great tale, pour a perfect cocktail, and, more importantly, cook. He always turns out something delicious and surprising, whether it's stuffed quail (New Year's Eve), chicken in ginger sauce (a weeknight in the city) or cheese soufflé (a contribution at my house where he brought his own soufflé dish and all the fixings). But this advertising executive comes from a long line of folks who loved to cook and entertain.

"My father was a Scot, my mother hailed from Jersey and my brother and I were brought up as very proper British boys. Every evening Dad, who was a doctor, would come home from the surgery, sip a glass of sherry with my mother, and we would all sit down to a beautifully laid table," says Iain. "The meal may have started with homemade soup, followed by something simple but robust like Shepherd's pie or lamb chops with vegetables, and ending with a pudding (the British word for dessert). So at a very early age I was exposed to good food served well. Takeout was never an option."

Since his parents often entertained, Iain was also exposed to fancier dishes and to the art of giving parties. He fondly remembers Hogmanay, a Scottish New Year's Eve celebration. "My brother Jack and I would go to sleep at our regular ➤

The Pages

TO DO

● Ribbed green scrapbook papers are the background for all the recipes, but squares of the clan tartan fabric on alternate pages snap things up. Just affix to the green papers with spray adhesive. On adjacent pages, use smaller bits of the tartan—a strip here, a bow there, a clever rosette along an edge—to create a sense of unity.
TIP To minimize cost, color-copy the fabric onto paper and use that to create your "fabric" swatches.

● Arrange photos and recipes in a pleasing arrangement, positioning additional ephemera such as maps, landscapes, envelopes, even old money, for more impact.

● Use black photo corners and small metal frames to highlight photos; place other adornments such as ribbons, dried flowers, and family pins as desired.
TIP Use a single-hole punch to make holes in recipes and thread ribbon through them; tie into a bow.

● Affix papers and most embellishments with glue dots; use rubber cement for metal frames.

Tuck tiny treasures and selected ephemera into small envelopes for a charming sense of secrecy.

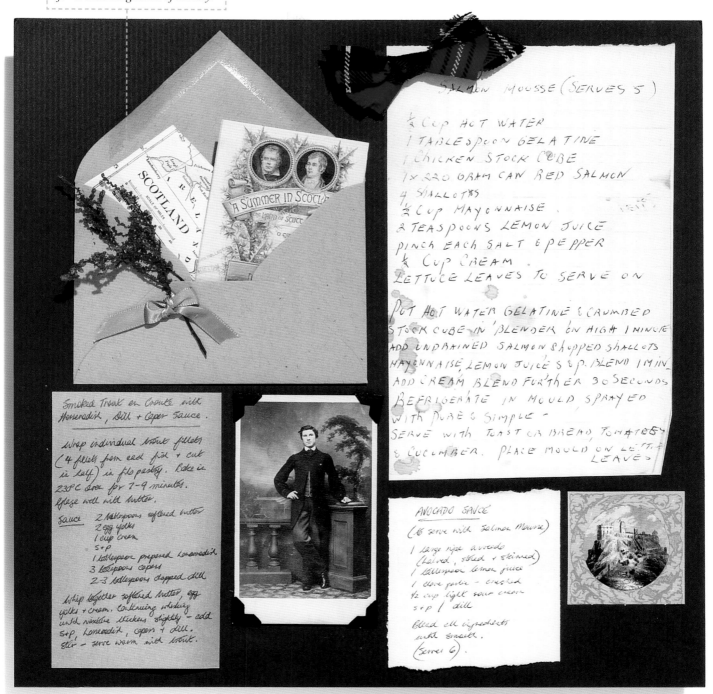

Handwritten recipes combined with vintage photos and newspaper clippings make flipping through the book a journey back in time.

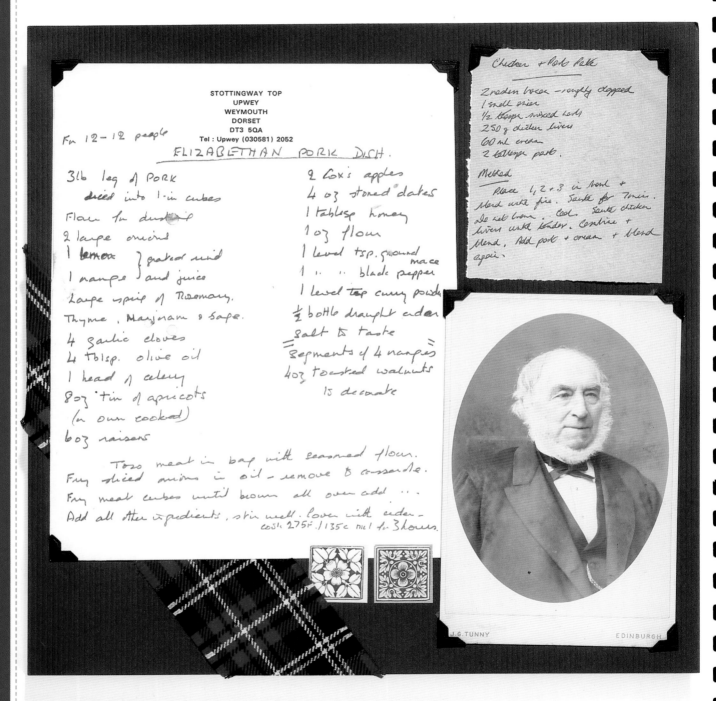

STOTTINGWAY TOP
UPWEY
WEYMOUTH
DORSET
DT3 5QA
Tel : Upwey (030581) 2052

For 12-18 people

ELIZABETHAN PORK DISH.

3lb leg of PORK
  diced into 1-in cubes
Flour for dusting
2 large onions
1 lemon ⎫ grated rind
1 orange ⎭ and juice
Large sprig of Rosemary,
Thyme, Marjoram & Sage.
4 garlic cloves
4 tblsp. olive oil
1 head of celery
8oz tin of apricots
(in own cooked)
6oz raisins

2 Cox's apples
4 oz stoned dates
1 tablsp honey
1 oz flour
1 level tsp. ground mace
1 .. .. blade pepper
1 level tsp curry powder
½ bottle draught cider
salt to taste
segments of 4 oranges
4oz toasted walnuts
to decorate

  Toss meat in bag with seasoned flour.
Fry sliced onions in oil - remove to casserole.
Fry meat cubes until brown all over add ...
Add all other ingredients, stir well. Cover with cider.
cook 275F. / 135c mk1 for 3 hours.

Chicken + Pork Pâté

2 rashers bacon - roughly chopped
1 small onion
½ tbspn mixed herbs
250 g chicken livers
60 ml cream
2 tablespn port.

Method

Place 1, 2 + 3 in bowl +
blend until fine. Sauté for 7min.
Do not brown. Cool. Sauté chicken
livers until tender. Combine +
blend. Add port + cream + blend
again.

J.G.TUNNY   EDINBURGH

Old fashioned photo corners are a natural for this project,
lending heirloom appeal to both snapshots and recipes.

Rules of attachment: For an engaging, homespun look, affix recipes to pages with straight pins.

Turnip soup

Serves 8.

6-8 young turnips peeled and sliced, 30 g butter, ½ tspn salt, ¼ tspn sugar, fine white pepper to taste, 6 cups chicken stock, 1 egg yolk, ¼ cup cream, freshly snipped chives or finely-chopped parsley to garnish.

Cook turnips in medium pan in butter stirring from time to time for five minutes. Add salt, sugar and pepper, stir and pour in stock. Simmer until turnips are soft. Either sieve or mouli the soup and return to the pan. Beat yolk with cream, stir into soup and heat through without boiling. Serve in warmed soup bowls and garnish with the herbs.

For spicy plum masala:
200g fresh red plums
100g sugar
100ml nut oil
1 lemongrass stick
(chopped fine)
5 small chillies
50ml red wine vinegar
2 tbsp chopped coriander

Place all the ingredients in a saucepan and cook for 20 minutes until the plums are completely soft. Once cooled, pass through a nylon sieve and season with sea salt.

Check your library for books with appropriate engravings and run off on a copier or scan into your computer. Look for landscapes, scenic buildings, fashions of the times.

Think of each page as a mini story, choosing photos
and adornments that enhance each other.

time, then be awakened just around midnight. We'd wash our faces, comb our hair and go downstairs in our pajamas. Everyone would be toasting and laughing and enjoying Scotch eggs or baked ham along with Stilton and pate and other goodies from the buffet. We'd say our hellos, have a snack, and then around 12:45 we were tucked back into bed again," recalls Iain with a smile.

This Scottish custom, which centers around the giving and receiving of gifts and the singing of "Auld Lang Syne," is just one Iain has brought with him to New York. Others include a Sunday supper featuring champagne and kedgeree (flaked fish, rice, eggs and butter, and actually quite good), the naming of his homes, wherever they may be, after towns in Scotland, and the wearing of the kilt to special celebrations. True to his heritage, Iain occasionally brings out traditional dishes like haggis (sheep's heart, liver and lungs boiled in the animal's stomach—not for me!), meat pies and oatcakes, and bread-and-butter pudding (always yummy).

Iain's recipes certainly deserved a better home, and his stories about his Scottish forebears got me thinking about lochs and castles and clan tartans. Iain is the beneficiary of an ancient velvet photo album filled with black-and-white portraits of solemn-looking ancestors—ladies and gents in stiff clothing and children dressed far too soberly for their young years. They stare directly at you from their oval slots on the parchment pages and one wonders what stories they could tell—and what they would say about life today. ➤

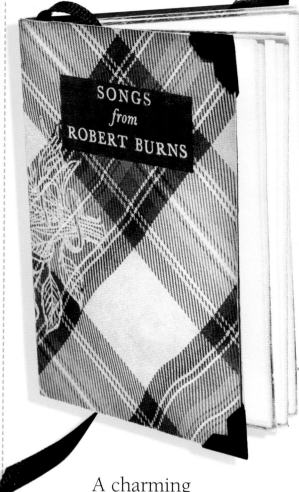

A charming mini-book of Scottish poems tucks into the album at the frontispiece, held in place by a black ribbon that doubles as a bookmark.

TECHNIQUE 101
Scale It Down

A miniature version of Iain's copy of *Songs from Robert Burns* makes a charming addition to the album.

Choose pages you want to reproduce and color-copy as double page spreads, putting a piece of white posterboard behind the pages.

Reduce to size desired. (We reduced our 4" x 6" pages by 60%.)

Color-copy front and back covers in the same way, but reduce by a little more to allow for some leeway when binding book together. (We used 65%.)

Trim the pages with a craft knife on a cutting board.

Score spreads with a bone folder. Collate and glue in order desired with spray adhesive.

Before gluing covers into place, use a small piece of tape to place a length of ¼-inch grosgrain ribbon between two of the pages.

Glue covers into place with spray adhesive.

Affix black photo corners on front and back covers.

Tuck ribbon into binding so readers can easily pull mini-book out.

Your mini-book could also be a collection of essays, fairy tales, even sheet music.

Armed with such glorious material, we put together this heritage cookbook, an album that offers a glimpse of Scottish history as well as a peek into the lives of the Hunter family. As I skimmed through it, the thought occurred to me that anyone could do a similar treatment, even without a slew of handed-down recipes. You could create your own store of recipes and customs just by doing some research on your own genealogy. Begin with a couple of well-loved dishes and go from there, supplementing the food with ethnic legends, poems and songs. Add any personal anecdotes you may uncover, and you'll have a one-of-a-kind album that's a fascinating read as well as an inspiring cookbook. As befits a coffee-table book, the cover is classy and classic—a family crest framed with leather sitting on a piece of the clan tartan. ■ ■ ■

Finishing Touches

TO DO

Sample frames are used throughout the pages to set off both recipes and photos. Find them at craft stores or create your own from patterned or wood-grained papers.

DIFFERENT TAKES

Rather than a map for your endpapers, color copy your family tree or place your ephemera on a piece of fabric. Add appropriate coins, buttons or charms for texture—anything that symbolizes something from your family history.

No crest? No problem. Blow up your family monogram or initial and use that as the focal point for the cover.

If you are not lucky enough to have old handwritten recipes, mimic the look by printing out recipes in different fonts. Try italic, handwriting, calligraphy or typewriter fonts and age your papers by brushing them with a weak tea solution, then drying and crumpling slightly.

SHIELD TEMPLATE

Recipes to Try

From crowd-pleasing main dishes to simple weeknight soups, these recipes will always find fans.

21st-Century Roast Chicken

Serves 4–6, depending on size of bird

● Iain has fond memories of his mother's roast chicken—a staple at the Hunter home—but these days he puts his own spin on it.

1 small roaster chicken

Ground black pepper and kosher salt to season

2 lemons

3 cloves garlic, peeled and crushed

Several sprigs fresh thyme

1 tablespoon butter, softened

Olive oil

Preheat oven to 400 degrees F.

Take a fresh, preferably organic chicken, wash and pat dry. Season inside cavity and skin with ground black pepper and kosher salt. Cut one lemon into quarters and place in the cavity, along with two cloves of crushed garlic and a couple of sprigs of fresh thyme.

Remove thyme leaves from rest of stems, chop roughly, mix with the remaining crushed garlic, and add to the butter, blending into a smooth paste.

With your fingers, gently release the skin from the body of the chicken and place the butter mixture under the skin, spreading it as evenly as possible

over the breast area.

In ovenproof dish, place chicken. Drizzle a little olive oil over chicken and roast for 40 minutes, basting often with more olive oil. Reduce temperature to 350 F, continuing to baste. Once skin begins to turn golden, squeeze the juice of one lemon over it.

Chicken will probably take 70–90 minutes, depending on size. To check for doneness, pierce thigh meat with a skewer; juices should run clear. Remove from oven, cover with foil and rest for 5 minutes before carving.

Serve with a green salad and roasted potatoes.

Blueberry & Cointreau Bread Pudding

Serves 6

● This is a little fancier than the version Iain grew up with, but it has the same homey goodness. You can experiment with different jams and berries—apricot jam and strawberries, perhaps, or for an intense raspberry hit, raspberry jam, raspberries and cassis instead of Cointreau.

6–8 croissants

Orange marmalade

1 pint fresh blueberries (or thawed, frozen blueberries)

1 cup milk

½ cup heavy cream

½–1 tablespoon Cointreau

2 eggs

2 tablespoons sugar

¼ teaspoon ground nutmeg

¼ teaspoon cinnamon

¼ teaspoon allspice

Preheat oven to 350 degrees F. Butter an oven-safe glass or ceramic baking dish.

Split the croissants lengthwise and spread with orange marmalade. Lay half of the croissant halves over bottom of baking dish; spoon blueberries over them. Then top with the rest of the croissants.

Whisk together milk, heavy cream, Cointreau, eggs, sugar and the spices.

Pour milk mixture gently over layered croissants, making sure mixture comes at least three-quarters up the dish. Push top croissants down to absorb mixture.

Place dish into a bain-marie of warm water. (Simply pour water into another larger baking dish so water comes halfway up side of oven dish.)

Place in preheated oven and cook for 45 minutes or until mixture is firm and a skewer is clean when inserted into pudding. (Cooking time will vary depending on size of dish.)

Remove from oven and let rest for 5 minutes. Serve with heavy cream or ice cream.

Shepherd's Pie

Serves 8

⬤ Nothing could be more British then Shepherd's Pie and this version is truly luscious—the ultimate comfort food

6 medium potatoes, peeled and roughly chopped

1 large onion, peeled and finely chopped

2 strips of bacon finely chopped

Olive oil as needed

2 lbs good quality ground beef

2 large carrots, peeled and finely diced

1 beef bouillon cube

Salt and pepper to taste

¼ cup milk

1 ounce butter

Preheat oven to 350 degrees F.

Rinse chopped potatoes to remove starch and then bring to boil in salted water in a medium saucepan. Cover and reduce to simmer until cooked through. Remove from heat and set aside.

While potatoes are cooking, in a medium saucepan, lightly saute onions and bacon together on medium heat, adding a little olive oil if necessary. Add ground beef and cook until browned, stirring occasionally. Add finely diced carrot, crumbled beef bouillon cube, salt and ground pepper to taste; stir and cover. Cook for 30 minutes, stirring a couple times. Remove from heat and cool.

Bring potatoes briefly back to the boil, remove from heat and drain well; return to pot. Mash the potatoes, adding about a quarter of a cup of milk and 1 ounce butter as you do so. When there are no lumps, take a wooden spoon and stir the potatoes vigorously—this "creams" the potato and gives a finer, smoother texture.

Into an ovenproof casserole dish, spoon all the slightly cooled ground beef mixture as a first layer. Add the mashed potato on top, using a fork to smooth out. Place uncovered in the oven and cook for 30 minutes. To finish, place casserole dish under broiler for a couple of minutes to brown the potato topping.

Serve immediately with a medley of steamed or stir-fried green vegetables.

Butternut Squash Soup

Serves 6

⬤ Always one to push the envelope, Iain's taken a classic family favorite and given it a distinctly Asian twist with the addition of chili garlic sauce and coconut milk.

1 ounce butter

1 medium onion, peeled and chopped

1 teaspoon chili garlic sauce

1 butternut squash, peeled and diced

1 large potato, peeled and diced

1 32-ounce carton chicken stock

1 blade lemon grass (optional)

Salt and ground pepper to taste

¼–½ cup coconut milk

Cilantro for garnish

In a medium-sized saucepan, melt butter on medium heat. Add chopped onion and stir until transparent. Add chili garlic sauce, combine with onion and then add squash, potato and chicken stock and bring to boil. If using lemon grass, add now. Reduce to a simmer, cover and cook for 30 minutes until vegetables are soft and flavors well rounded. Remove lemon grass.

With a handheld mixer or immersion blender, puree mixture until smooth. Add salt and ground pepper to taste and add ¼ cup coconut milk. Stir and taste, adjusting seasonings and add more coconut milk if desired. Stir and heat as necessary. Serve garnished with cilantro.

Soup can be refrigerated for about a week or frozen.

Note: Iain uses Tuong Ot Toi Vietnamese Chili Garlic Sauce by Huy Fong Foods which he buys in New York City's Chinatown. An 18- ounce jar costs about $2, lasts forever and is excellent in curries, stir fries and anytime you wish to add a delicious chili warmth to sauces and marinades.Similar products are available in the Asian section of most supermarkets.

Here's a present that's pretty and practical: a custom box filled with go-to recipes and cooking tips.

Here Comes the Bride

BRIDE'S RECIPE BOX

I was at a bridal shower recently, and as we all watched the bride opening her gifts, I wondered just how this custom began. A little research turned up…very little! Most theories say the ritual started as a simple get-together for the bride and her friends, a sort of girls'-night-out party where advice was traded and friendship celebrated. It wasn't until the late 1800s that gifts were exchanged. A popular custom back then was to place small presents inside a parasol, so once the parasol was opened there would be a "shower" of gifts. Oddly enough, an old Dutch legend credits the groom's friends for the gifting, not the bride's. But these days, with couples' showers so popular, it hardly seems to matter.

What does matter, however, is giving a memorable gift, something apart from the usual. Charitable donations are a trend many new brides are embracing. So are contributions toward a big-ticket item. But a one-of-a-kind keepsake is always appreciated, and that's where *Cookbooking* comes in. You could put together a book of your own go-to recipes or collect different versions of the bride's favorite dishes. She's nuts about seafood? Compile a small album of variations and present it with a gift card to a nearby ▶

:For:

PATTIE

Om Alyson... Stacey Tricia

Our Bride's Box is at once feminine
and fun, a spritely cache for recipes
and mementos that can take pride of
place on the cookbook shelf.

131

GET THE LOOK
The Box

TO DO

- Select two sheets of cardstock, one for the outside of the box (ours is lime) and one as a liner (ours is brown) as well as a piece of posterboard.

- Follow the steps in Technique 101 to shape the box.

- Affix button on lid by poking fine wire through the buttonholes and through all three layers. Twist wire to fasten securely; clip ends. Place a piece of masking tape over wire.

- Select another color of cardstock (ours is lavender) for nameplate and draw appropriate shape to fit lid of box. Cut out with craft knife. Emboss with the same design as the front of the box.

- Spell out "For [Bride's Name]" with rub-on letters.

- Affix nameplate to inside lid with spray adhesive.

TECHNIQUE 101
Out of the Box

According to Pattie, making a box is easier than you think, especially if you have the template—and you do!

Before you start, lay down a craft foam mat as a work surface. This will make cutting and scoring easier.

Trace template (page 128) onto the two pieces of cardstock and the posterboard.

Cut all three pieces to fit template with a craft knife.

Stack pieces on top of each other just to make certain all edges line up.

Score all three pieces separately, as indicated on template, using a bone folder.

Emboss the outside sheet of cardstock (in our case, the lime) using an embossing kit. We used a simple scroll design, but almost anything will do. (When you do this, be sure to emboss the top side of the cardstock, not the side that faces in.)

Glue posterboard to back side of cardstock with a spray adhesive, making certain edges and creases line up perfectly. Glue the brown liner onto that, using a spray adhesive. Crease again. Let dry.

Fold into shape, once again using bone folder to keep creases crisp.

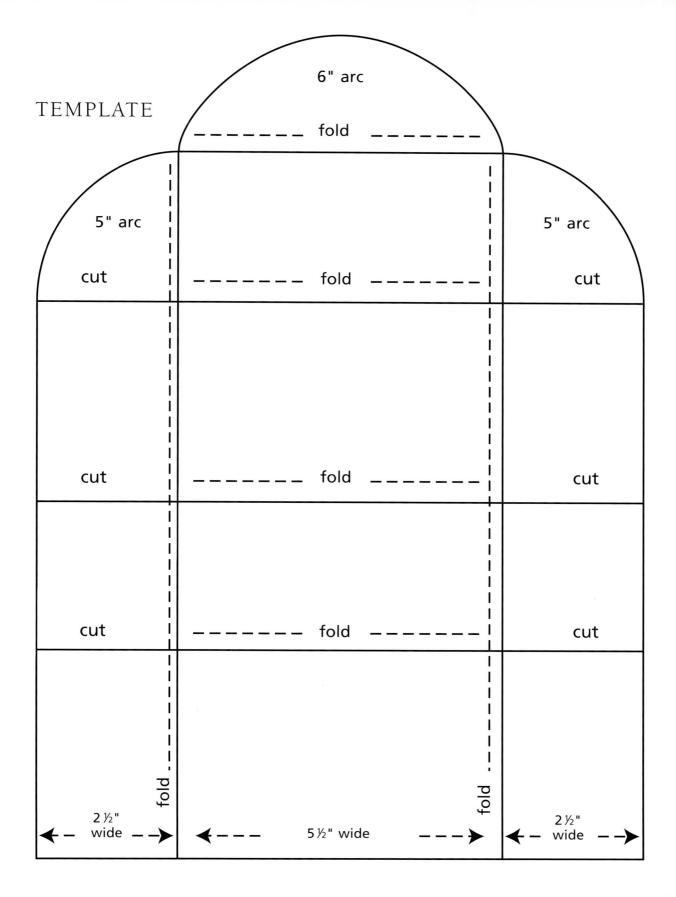

TEMPLATE

6" arc

fold

5" arc

5" arc

cut

fold

cut

cut

fold

cut

cut

fold

cut

cut

cut

fold

fold

2 ½"
wide

5 ½" wide

2 ½"
wide

restaurant. Or collect a series of recipes for her top-rated cuisine, accompanied by appropriate ingredients—Japanese, for instance, with wasabi, ponzu and sake. Or consider our Bride's Box, a very chic cache of recipes from her bridesmaids (or friends, or family, or whomever). The idea is to fashion a one-of-a-kind box and to give coordinating blank cards to each contributor. Each person writes up a recipe or two and you put them all in the box, neatly organized according to the giver's name.

Sentimental, yes, but smart too.

THE INSPIRATION

This project is a collaboration of many minds. The idea began over lunch with my friend Barbara Carlin, who, when she heard about *Cookbooking*, immediately said, "You have to do something for a new bride." She was thinking of her soon-to-be-married niece Emi, but every bride needs a stockpile of easy, reliable recipes. Then, Art Director Diane Lamphron took things a step further when she declared, "Not a book—a box." Book Editor Elaine Silverstein chimed in with "What a great shower gift." That prompted me to envision shower guests writing out recipes on blank cards to fit the box. Designer Pattie Donham happens to make marvelous boxes, so she set out to concoct one that's a real inspiration.

Assembling your own Bride's Box is another case of collaboration. One person should make the box and the cards, and another take charge of ➤

The Dividers

TO DO

- Select polka-dot papers to meld with the color palette; cut to size.

- Cut either black or solid papers to the same size and affix to the polka dots with a glue stick to give the dividers more heft.

- Cut small circles—a little larger than a quarter—from coordinating solid papers. (These will act as index tabs identifying the names of the givers.)

- Spell out name of giver with rub-on letters.
TIP You can also do this with a paint or calligraphy pen if you have a knack for lettering.

- Affix circles to top edge of each divider with a glue stick, making sure they are staggered so all the names can be seen within the box.

DIFFERENT TAKES

Any number of coordinating papers will change the look of the box completely. Choose glittery or metallic papers, Victorian patterns, florals, or any pattern you love. Two lines we especially like: Martha Stewart (the Candy Shop, Spring Parade and Café multipacks offer fun but sophisticated patterns) and K'ology (mix the Peabody and Verbena collections together for an updated vintage look).

Ditch the ribbon and consider a fabric frog as an elegant fastener for your box. Scout out the selection at a fabric or trimmings store, then just glue into place. Or, try two small buttons held together with a colored elastic loop.

Play around with different shapes for your index tabs—rectangles, triangles, scallops—making sure they're large enough to accommodate a person's name. Or purchase personalized paper clips to attach to the divider cards. Ovals, arrows and rectangles are just some of the shapes available; any would add a playful touch to the box.

Colorful circle tags sit atop the perky polka-dot dividers, calling attention to each contributor's recipes.

from Stacey

from Tricia

from Alyson

sending out the blank cards along with the shower invitations. Depending on the number of people involved, each guest should get one or two cards. Instructions are simple; just write or print out a no-fail recipe. Contributors can embellish their cards with drawings, stickers, charms, whatever, but just writing down the recipe is enough. Pattie did offer this thought, however: "If you know certain people aren't crafty, include a doodad of some sort on their cards. It will make things look prettier." Guests drop off their cards at the beginning of the shower, and all that's needed is a few minutes to organize them in the box. Present to the bride nestled into a gift basket laden with gourmet goodies or kitchen gadgets.

A few more details that might make the box even better:

● Depending on the cooking prowess of the bride, you can include cards with tips: how to make eggs (hard- and soft-boiled, fried, poached and so on), whip up a basic vinaigrette, make gravy, cook a steak, etc.

● Put in some coupons or gift cards for local restaurants. Or, tuck in a card with "emergency" takeout numbers for Chinese, pizza, etc.

● Include some bartender specials: recipes for classic cocktails (you never know when she'll need them), along with a list of good wine choices.

● Tuck in a subscription card marked "On the Way" for a cooking magazine: *Bon Appetit*, *Gourmet*, *Food and Wine*, or *Cooking Light* are ➤

The Cards

TO DO

● Select coordinating pieces of scrapbook paper in a color palette that suits the bride. We chose pink, aqua and lavender—a perfect complement to our lime and brown box.

● Cut papers to fit box. Ours are 5½" x 3¼".

● Cut sheets of white paper just a bit smaller and affix to the paper cards with a glue stick so a colored border is seen all around.

● Cut small circles from the scrapbook papers, the same color as the borders, and affix to corners of some of the cards as an embellishment.
TIP Leave some circles blank so people can write comments on them; accent others with stickers or charms.

SPECIAL GEAR
Embossing tools and kits can be found at most craft stores: **Fiskars** produces starter kits that contain stencil designs and a dual-tip stylus.

These simple cards
with colored borders
are given to friends and
family to fill out with
their favorite recipes.

Chow Chow
1 Peck Green Tomatoes (12½ lbs.)
8 Large Onions
3 tbs. Salt   10 Green Bell Peppers
1 Quart Vinegar   6 Hot Peppers
¼ tsp. Allspice   1 tbs. Cinnamon
3 tbs. mustard   ¼ tsp. Cloves
4 or 5 lbs. Cabbage   Few Bay
Cook until tender.
seal. We love
beans in

♥ Stacey

Lemonade Stand Pie
1 can frozen Lemonade, soft
1 Pint vanilla ice cream, soft
8 oz. thawed whipped topping
1 graham cracker crust

Beat lemonade on low for 30 secs. Spoon in the
ice cream until blended. Gently stir in whipped
topping. Spoon into crust. Freeze 4 hours
Let   room temp for 30 min & eat
Ba   Freeze leftovers---not! ☺

- We
- love
- this!
- Tricia

Crock Pot Potatoes............from Alyson
1 (16-oz.) pkg. frozen broccoli cuts
1 lb. cooked ham, diced 1 medium onion,
1 jalapeño pepper, chopped
1 can cream of celery soup
4 to 6 large baking potatoes

Put broccoli, slightly thawed, into slow cooker. Add ham, onion, jalapeño
pepper and cream of celery soup. Cook on Low for 4 hours. Bake potatoes,
either in microwave or oven, and when baked, split in half. Using slotted
spoon, spoon slow-cooked mixture into potatoes and garnish with toppers
of choice, such as bacon bits, shredded cheese, green onions, etc.

the classics, but *Every Day with Rachael Ray, Saveur, Fine Cooking, Cook's Illustrated* and *Everyday Food* are also excellent suggestions. Specialized publications are fun too: consider *Chile Pepper, Herb Companion, La Cucina Italiana* and *Vegetarian Times.*

● Jot down some helpful cooking websites: we love foodnetwork.com, epicurious.com, starchefs.com and recipehound.com. But check with friends for their recommendations.

How could any bride not love this? ■ ■ ■

GET THE LOOK
Finishing Touches

TO DO

● Cut a length of narrow ribbon long enough to wrap around box with a few inches left over. We picked brown with little white dashes to pick up the color of the box lining.

● Affix to box with glue stick.

● Make a bow from another piece of the ribbon and affix to center front of box, on top of the strand of ribbon you already glued into place.

● Cut a circle from one of your scrapbook papers to fit inside a blank metal tag. Affix circle to tag with a glue stick.

● Draw the bride's initial from another piece of scrapbook paper, using a stencil or alphabet font as a guide. Cut out and glue onto tag. Tie onto ribbon bow with a small piece of embroidery floss.

● Close box by tucking lid inside and winding extra bit of ribbon around button.

Our nifty little box is feminine, but fun, a sprightly catchall for recipes in lime and brown with a splash of lavender.

Recipes to Try

Cajun Cornish Hens

Serves 2

● You can't go wrong with Cornish hens: They're great roasted or grilled with just an herb butter for basting and take beautifully to all kinds of rubs and glazes. Served with couscous or a rice pilaf and salad, this recipe makes a simple but elegant dinner..

2 Cornish hens

Kosher salt

1 small lemon, halved

6 sprigs fresh thyme

½ tablespoon herbes de Provence

1 ½ tablespoons Cajun seasoning

½ tablespoon chili powder

2–3 tablespoons Worchestershire sauce

1 tablespoon butter (for basting)

Preheat oven to 400 degrees F.

Wash and thoroughly dry the Cornish hens. Sprinkle cavities with kosher salt, then place half a lemon and a few sprigs of thyme in each cavity.

Mix the herbes de Provence, Cajun seasoning and chili powder together and rub over the hens, making sure all skin is covered with the spices.

Place hens breast-side up in a baking dish and pour Worchestershire sauce over.

Place pats of butter on hens.

Bake at 400 F for 15 minutes; lower heat to 350 F and cook for 45 minutes. (Turn hens over after 15 minutes at 350 F or when breast skin is golden brown.) Hens are done when juices run clear.

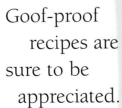

Goof-proof recipes are sure to be appreciated.

Pork Chops with Two Mustards

Serves 2

● The secret here is twofold: English mustard, which is much spicier than brown or Dijon varieties, and the fennel seeds, which impart a subtle tang.

1 ½ tablespoons Dijon-style mustard

1 ½ tablespoons English-style mustard (Coleman's is preferred)

1 tablespoon olive oil

½ tablespoon crushed fennel seeds

½ tablespoon herbes de Provence

Salt and pepper to taste

2 center cut pork chops, about 2 inches thick

Preheat oven to 375 degrees F.

Mix the mustards, olive oil, fennel and herbs together into a thin paste (add more oil if necessary). Season the pork chops with salt and pepper, then spread the mustard mixture over both sides of each chop. Allow to marinate about 20 minutes.

Place chops in baking dish and cook for about 30 minutes, occasionally basting with the mustard sauce. Chops are finished when meat is white through and through.

Serve immediately, spooning any sauce from baking dish onto the chops.

Ways and Means

RESOURCES FOR COOKBOOKING

By now, even those of you who aren't crafters or scrapbookers have probably familiarized yourself with some new techniques and tools. But if something still needs clearing up, take a look at these pages. They'll clue you in the basic gear and give you tips to make your efforts more rewarding.

TOOLS OF THE TRADE

In the same way that pots and pans and kitchen gadgets are necessary for any cook to do her best job, there are certain supplies that will make your *Cookbooking* projects go easier and look better. Most are very inexpensive and can be found in the scrapbooking section of craft stores, some at stationery supply stores. To familiarize yourself with what's around, you might want to do a general web search for "scrapbooking supplies" or zero in on a specific type of product (e.g. scrapbook papers).

THE BASICS

Albums Usually available in four styles—three-ring binder, spiral, post or strap bound and in a variety of materials from leather to canvas to paper to plastic. Most popular sizes are 12" x 12" and 8" x 8", but other sizes such as 6" x 6" and 8.5" x 11" are out there.

Scrapbook papers These are available in limitless colors, patterns and textures. They are sold as single sheets, packets or booklets with the most common sizes being 12" x 12" and 8" x 8". Sometimes you can find 12" x 15", but if you want something smaller, you will probably need to cut it yourself. Variety packs are another interesting option.

Page protectors Transparent sleeves cover and protect cookbooking pages. Many sizes and styles are produced, but top-loading ones are your best option. Look for those that are non-reactive PVC-free plastic.

Adhesives There's a wealth of adhesives around, from tiny "glue dots" sold in packets to paper pastes in bottles. Most of the projects in this book use glue dots (for affixing embellishments), glue sticks (for photos, cards and recipes) and spray adhesive (for fabric and large pieces of paper or cardstock). You might also want to purchase an adhesive remover to clean up any mistakes. (A favorite of crafters is Un-Du.)

Cutting Tools You will definitely need a craft knife (this usually comes with replacement blades) and a pair of good paper scissors with comfort-grip handles. A couple of decorative scissors (these will give you pretty pinked, scalloped or rickrack edges) are also nice to have on hand. Hole punches (single and three-hole) are a good idea for forming neat holes in papers and cardstock.

Pens, pencils, markers It depends on the effect you want, but pigment pens are a good all-purpose choice. They come in a huge range of colors and tip widths; just make sure yours are light-fast, fade-resistant, waterproof and colorfast. Scouting out the craft store will reveal all sorts of other choices, from glitter pens to gel pens to vanishing ink pens.

THE EXTRAS

Paper trimmer Sometimes called a personal or portable paper trimmer, these compact gadgets cut papers to size precisely and quickly, assuring a straight, clean edge. Some come with an attached measuring grid.

Stencil template You can't beat a stencil for spelling out emphatic titles, so you may want to purchase an alphabet template kit. These usually include a template of the 26 letters in the font of your choice, along with a cutting mat, swivel knife and scoring tool.

Corner punches These nifty little gadgets shape corners on papers with just the press of a finger. A round-corner punch is an ideal deal (around $4) to give a finished look to recipe pages, but a few more dollars will buy you other patterns such as basketweave, floral or scallop.

Happy Cookbooking!

MAKE IT PERSONAL

Part of the fun of cookbooking is adding your own individual touch, whether it be a series of store-bought stickers that play up the theme of your album or a fun way to create a border. Here are some suggestions for giving a personal spin to some popular adornments.

EMBELLISHMENTS

This term encompasses everything from whimsical stickers to self-sticking foam shapes to the miniature bottlecap letters on our Breakfast Tin. Check out the web or stop by your local craft store and you'll discover scads of premades. Some come in kits; others are available in separate packets, and all are designed to make your cookbooking pages shine with personality. They'll also give you ideas for your own embellishments. Once you've done some scouting, scour your own closets and drawers for items like:

Tags Plain manila ones complete with their string are nice places to jot a comment or title on your cookbooking pages. Just affix with a glue stick. Or use small metal-rimmed tags to indicate the prep time needed for a recipe.

Buttons Perfect in a row or a cluster, or solo as an attractive touch on a plain computer printout (see "Home for the Holidays" album).

Beads A simple row is an interesting way to underline a title, or glue into a starburst shape to act as a 3-D asterisk, or combine with yarn for a multimedia effect.

Charms An easy way to add instant whimsy.

Ribbons Nothing beats them for borders—or tie into bows and use to anchor photos or recipes. You can also transform them into index tabs as Pattie Donham did on her mom's Memory Book.

Colored ponytail bands Loop a few together for a neat embellishment at the corner of a page, or snip into strands and use as "squiggles."

Paper clips Glue into place on a recipe for a trompe l'oeil effect.

STENCILS AND STAMPS

Alphabet stencils and stamps are one of the easiest ways to highlight pages with distinctive words or titles, but think beyond applying directly to your page or cover. Try these tricks:

- Stencil or stamp letters onto a torn piece of colored paper, then affix to page with glue stick.

- Stencil or stamp letters onto small, equally sized squares of paper to spell out a title. Affix to page. For a more playful effect, make the squares different sizes and use different fonts.

- Stamp simple images like circles, squares, suns or stars directly onto pages, then stamp appropriate words within the image. For instance, for a party book, you might stamp stars and do words within them like "fun", "enjoy", "party", "celebrate". (Instead of stamping the words, you could also write freehand). Or, combine stamped images with stickers.

BORDERS

Even simple computer printouts will gain an edge with an interesting border treatment.

- Make an easy striped border by cutting four narrow strips of paper in different colors. Mount along all four sides of your cookbook page and then glue recipes within the border.

- Take yarn, raffia or string and glue several strips to bottom or side of recipe. For an even jazzier effect, affix on a slant or crisscross here and there. Or, even simpler, just create a straight all-around border.

- With pinking shears or decorative scissors, cut a piece of fabric a little larger than your recipe. Center recipe on fabric and glue down. Then, affix to page with spray adhesive.

DO SOME JOURNALING

In scrapbooking, the term "journaling" refers to any text written by the scrapbooker. It can range from a short, descriptive label to fairly extensive copy about an event or photo. This sharing of information is necessary so that people can leaf through the scrapbook and understand the pages without the presence of the author.

Cookbooking needs less explanatory text, but you may want to "journal" additional recipe information, add a thought about a particular menu, record a tip about how to serve a dish. Here are some ways to do this:

- Make a comment: Print lively quotes or quick comments onto strips of vellum, choosing a color for the type that works with your background page. Attach small pieces of twisted yarn or knotted ribbon onto the left top corner of the vellum and affix to page so it hangs like a tag. You could also write directly onto the vellum with a paint pen.

- Capture a caption: Print small blocks of text onto solid or subtly patterned paper, then cut to size and rim the edges with black or colored pen. Affix to page with adhesive. (This works best for text of 25–40 words).

- Highlight a quote: Print a quote on coordinating paper in black type, but call attention to certain words by putting them in a larger or bolder font or in a different color. Affix onto background page.

- Tell a story: Sometimes the story behind the meal is as interesting as the meal itself! Print text onto a square of solid paper, then use a black or colored pen to draw in a border. Mount onto a slightly larger square of patterned paper. Affix to page. Finish off by attaching a colored or swirled paper clip at one corner. This is also a swell way to showcase a menu or a guest list.

ACKNOWLEDGMENTS

A very special thanks to Pattie Donham, craftsperson extraordinaire, who executed most of the projects in this book and brought her wit, charm and imagination to everything you see; a heartfelt thank you to Michael Kraus for taking such time and care with the photography; much appreciation to Gina Norgard for testing the recipes and contributing some of her own marvelous dishes; enormous thanks to Gloria Tracey for her inspiring design and Joan Fee for her marvelous ideas; a hug to my friends Janice, Lindsay, Barbara, John and Tom for their support and advice, and especially to Iain and Cathleen, who provided such a treasure trove of material; and, of course, thank you to all the people at Sixth&Spring Books, especially Art Director Diane Lamphron, who went the extra mile, and Wendy Williams, who came in midway with grace and patience, and Trisha Malcolm and Art Joinnides, who said "Go for it."

ABOUT THE AUTHOR

Barbara Winkler is the former executive editor of *Family Circle* magazine, where her work with food, crafts and decorating gave her the inspiration for this book. Like many women, she had recipes stashed in various drawers, boxes and folders and could never put her hands on the ones she needed. Drawing on her experience with stylists and designers, she took the concept of scrapbooking and turned it into *Cookbooking.* Now she actually looks forward to entertaining in her 1750 farmhouse in Connecticut. When she's not cooking, gardening or trying to turn trash into treasure (she loves street finds and flea market bargains), Barbara is likely to be working on a soon-to-be-published book about New York restaurant chefs or writing articles about food, home and gardens for national publications.